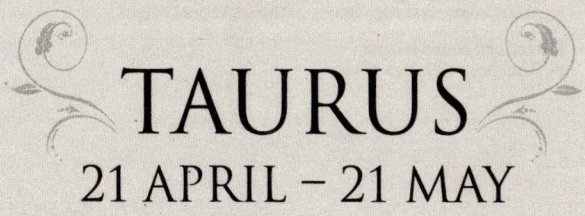

TAURUS
21 APRIL – 21 MAY

DID YOU PURCHASE THIS BOOK WITHOUT A COVER?

If you did, you should be aware it is **stolen property** as it was reported *unsold and destroyed* by a retailer. Neither the author nor the publisher has received any payment for this book.

All Rights Reserved including the right of reproduction in whole or in part in any form. This edition is published by arrangement with Harlequin Enterprises II B.V./S.à.r.l. The text of this publication or any part thereof may not be reproduced or transmitted in any form or by any means, electronic or mechanical, including photocopying, recording, storage in an information retrieval system, or otherwise, without the written permission of the publisher.

This book is sold subject to the condition that it shall not, by way of trade or otherwise, be lent, resold, hired out or otherwise circulated without the prior consent of the publisher in any form of binding or cover other than that in which it is published, and without a similar condition including this condition being imposed on the subsequent purchaser.

® and ™ are trademarks owned and used by the trademark owner and/or its licensee. Trademarks marked with ® are registered with the United Kingdom Patent Office and/or the Office for Harmonisation in the Internal Market and in other countries.

First published in Great Britain 2011
by Mills & Boon, an imprint of Harlequin (UK) Limited,
Eton House, 18-24 Paradise Road, Richmond, Surrey TW9 1SR

Copyright © Dadhichi Toth 2011

ISBN: 978 0 263 89652 7

Design by Jo Yuen Graphic Design
Typeset by KDW DESIGNS

Harlequin (UK) policy is to use papers that are natural, renewable and recyclable products and made from wood grown in sustainable forests. The logging and manufacturing processes conform to the legal environmental regulations of the country of origin.

Printed and bound in Spain
by Blackprint CPI, Barcelona

Dedicated to

The Light of Intuition

Sri V. Krishnaswamy—mentor and friend

With thanks to

Joram and Isaac

Special thanks to

Nyle Cruz for

initial creative layouts and ongoing support

ABOUT DADHICHI

Dadhichi is one of Australia's foremost astrologers and is frequently seen on television and in other media. He has the unique ability to draw from complex astrological theory to provide clear, easily understandable advice and insights for people who want to know what their futures may hold.

In the 26 years that Dadhichi has been practising astrology, face reading and other esoteric studies, he has conducted over 10,000 consultations. His clients include celebrities, political and diplomatic figures, and media and corporate identities from all over the world.

Dadhichi's unique blend of astrology and face reading helps people fulfil their true potential. His extensive experience practising Western astrology is complemented by his research into the theory and practice of Eastern forms of astrology.

Dadhichi has been a guest on many Australian television shows, and several of his political and worldwide forecasts have proved uncannily accurate. He appears regularly on Australian television networks and is a columnist for online and offline Australian publications.

His websites—www.dadhichi.com and www.facereader.com—attract hundreds of thousands of visitors each month, and offer a wide variety of features, helpful information and services.

MESSAGE FROM DADHICHI

Hello once again and welcome to your 2012 horoscope book!

Can you believe it's already 2012? Time flies by so quickly and now here we are in this fateful year, a time for which several religions of the world—including the Mayans from 3100BC—have predicted some extraordinary events that are supposedly going to affect us all!

Some people are worried there will be a physical cataclysm that will kill millions and millions. Some are of the opinion it is the end of the economic and social models we have lived by for thousands of years. Others seem to believe the Planet Nibiru will whiz by planet Earth and beam up the 144,000 Chosen Ones.

Whatever the opinion, it is an undeniable fact that we are experiencing some remarkable worldwide changes due to global warming (even though that remains a point of contention) and other societal shifts. Scientific knowledge continues to outrun our ability to keep up with it, and time appears to be moving faster and faster.

But my own research has categorically led me to repeat: 'Relax, everyone; it is *not* the end of the world!' There will most certainly be a backlash at some point by Mother Earth at the gross unconsciousness of many of us. There will be ravaging storms, earthquakes and other meteorological phenomena that will shake the Earth, hopefully waking up those of us still in a deep sleep, dreaming, or possibly even sleepwalking. It is time to open our eyes and take responsibility.

If there are any significant global changes I foresee, they are the emergence of wider self-government and the greater Aquarian qualities of the coming New Age. This period is the cusp or changeover between the Age of Pisces, the Fish, and the Age of Aquarius, the Dawn of Higher Mankind.

Astrology, and these small books I write about it, are for the sole purpose of shedding light on our higher selves, alerting us to the need to evolve, step up to the plate, and assume responsibility for our thoughts, words and deeds, individually and collectively. The processes of karma are ripe now as we see the Earth's changes shouting to us about our past mistakes as a civilisation.

I hope you gain some deeper insight into yourself through these writings. For the 2012 series I have extended the topics and focused more on relationships. It is only through having a clear perception of our responsibility towards others that we can live the principles of astrology and karma to reach our own self-actualisation, both as individuals and as a race.

I hope you see the light of truth within yourself and that these words will act as a pointer in your ongoing search.

All the best for 2012.

Your Astrologer,

www.dadhichi.com
dadhichitoth@gmail.com
Tel: +61 (0) 413 124 809

CONTENTS

Taurus Profile

Taurus Snapshot	12
Taurus Overview	15
Taurus Cusps	18
Taurus Celebrities	22

Taurus at Large

Taurus Man	28
Taurus Woman	32
Taurus Child	35
Taurus Lover	37
Taurus Friend	40
Taurus Enemy	42

Taurus at Home

Home Front	46
Karma, Luck and Meditation	49
Health, Wellbeing and Diet	51
Finance Finesse	53

CONTENTS

Taurus at Work

Taurus Career	56
Taurus Boss	58
Taurus Employee	60
Professional Relationships: Best and Worst	62

Taurus in Love

Romantic Compatibility	68
Horoscope Compatibility for Taurus	72
Taurus Partnerships	78
Platonic Relationships: Best and Worst	82
Sexual Relationships: Best and Worst	86
Quiz: Have You Found Your Perfect Match?	91

2012: Yearly Overview

Key Experiences	98
Romance and Friendship	99
Work and Money	102
Health, Beauty and Lifestyle	109
Karma, Spirituality and Emotional Balance	114

CONTENTS
CONTINUED

2012: Monthly and Daily Predictions

January	118
February	125
March	132
April	138
May	145
June	151
July	158
August	164
September	170
October	176
November	182
December	188

2012: Astronumerology

The Power Behind Your Name	196
Your Planetary Ruler	203
Your Planetary Forecast	205

TAURUS
PROFILE

THINGS TURN OUT BEST FOR THOSE
WHO MAKE THE BEST OF THE WAY
THINGS TURN OUT.

Jack Buck

TAURUS SNAPSHOT

Key Life Phrase	I Possess
Zodiac Totem	The Bull
Zodiac Symbol	♉
Zodiac Facts	Second sign of the zodiac; fixed, fruitful, feminine and moist
Zodiac Element	Earth
Key Characteristics	Security conscious, resolute, sensual, dependable, faithful, secure, proud, obstinate and decisive
Compatible Star Signs	Virgo, Gemini, Cancer, Capricorn, Pisces and Aries
Mismatched Signs	Leo, Libra, Scorpio, Sagittarius and Aquarius

Ruling Planet		Venus
Love Planets		Mercury and Mars
Finance Planet		Mercury
Speculation Planet		Mercury
Career Planets		Saturn and Uranus
Spiritual and Karmic Planets		Saturn
Friendship Planet		Neptune and Jupiter
Destiny Planet		Mercury
Famous Taureans		Al Pacino, Penélope Cruz, Shirley MacLaine, Cate Blanchett, Renée Zellweger, Saddam Hussein, Kirsten Dunst, James Brown, George Clooney, Janet Jackson, Carmen Electra, David Beckham, Yehudi Menuhin, Jack Nicholson, Barbra Streisand, Carol Burnett, Uma Thurman, Joe Lewis, Cher and Andie MacDowell

Lucky Numbers and Significant Years	5, 6, 8, 14, 15, 17, 23, 24, 26, 32, 33, 35, 41, 42, 44, 50, 51, 53, 59, 60, 62, 68, 69, 77 and 80
Lucky Gems	Diamond, quartz crystal, aquamarine, lapis lazuli and emerald
Lucky Fragrances	Sandalwood, jasmine and rose
Affirmation/Mantra	I am secure and without need
Lucky Days	Wednesday, Friday and Saturday

TAURUS OVERVIEW

You are extremely loyal in your affections and friendships, so people immediately see in you a person who calls a spade a spade and doesn't beat around the bush. At times you are a little shy and must learn that it's okay to speak up, even if others don't agree with what you have to say. You are honest and will stick to your word once you have given a commitment to another.

Tenacity, endurance and loyalty are some of the key characteristics that typify you, Taurus. But not everyone finds it easy to live with you, because you have a very particular way of wanting things done. This sometimes sets others against you, but it doesn't bother you. Once you've made up your mind, you stick to your guns, even if someone gives you good reason to rethink your decision.

You love the finer things in life and enjoy the best that money can buy. Sometimes this is detrimental to your health and wellbeing, so you must always moderate your cravings for food, drink and excesses of any kind.

Because Taurus is an earth sign, you are grounded and generally see things from a practical angle. You don't have time for airy-fairy, hare-brained schemes, and, being branded a conservative stick in the mud, you prefer the tried and tested—with a known outcome—to risking everything on some shaky venture.

SECRET TAURUS...

You secretly fear poverty and having to rely on others. This is why you work so hard, always considering what the future has to bring and how you can manage a safe and secure future for you and your family. This approach is fine, but don't let it dominate your life so much that you forget to stop and smell the roses on the way.

You find it hard dealing with situations in which others call the shots. In a submissive position, you may need to eat humble pie for a while, but this will certainly not last long: you prefer to be in charge of your own finances and destiny. However, there are some Taureans who become lazy and end up in states that create great disharmony. If you have a goal, you should always go for it and be the master of your own destiny.

Although you are ambitious in your own way, you never rush to the finishing line. The old adage of 'slow and steady wins the race' is a perfect representation of the way you live your life. You may not be the first to achieve your goals, but when you finally reach your destination, you do so in a way that doesn't jeopardise other aspects of your life. Generally, people born under Taurus are not speculators or gamblers with life.

Plodding Taurus

You just won't be rushed or pushed by anyone, will you, Taurus? You must do things at a steady pace and on your own terms. In this way, you ensure that things are done in the correct fashion. You hate to see things prepared in a roughshod manner, and in many ways this will be a point of contention in your life. You strive to perfect the work you do.

You are an extremely patient person and have a great deal of compassion. You're able to help others see through their problems, because you're not caught up in the intellectual complexities that go hand-in-hand with complicated life scenarios. You are very impartial when listening to another person's point of view, even if you don't always agree. This is one of the things that endears you to others. Perseverance, a genuine listening ear, and a quiet, caring nature are some of the additional personality traits that make Taurus stand out from the rest.

TAURUS CUSPS

ARE YOU A CUSP BABY?

Being born on the changeover of two star signs means you have the qualities of both. Sometimes you don't know whether you're Arthur or Martha, as they say! Some of my clients can't quite figure out if they are indeed their own star sign, or the one before, or after. This is to be expected because being born on the borderline means you take on aspects of both. The following outlines give an overview of the subtle effects of these cusp dates and how they affect your personality quite significantly.

Taurus–Aries Cusp

You are fiercely independent, having the additional character traits of the sign of Aries. Aries is the one previous to yours, and if you were born between the 21st and the 28th of April, you will exhibit many of the traits of the Ram.

As well as having the fiery aspects of the Martian sign Aries, you are dependable and somewhat stubborn, although always extremely reliable and loyal. You have an ability to express your creative desires with great energy and persuasion. You have immense amounts of energy to achieve your objectives. However, no one should ever cross you, because you have a combative and explosive streak to your nature as well.

Aries-born individuals are very outspoken, so you will always speak your mind, even if, for others, this is uncomfortable. Because you have such a high level of Mars energy, your drive and your demands on people around you may be a little hard for them to cope with.

You will always have money, making a point to strive hard to achieve financial success and independence. Even if, in the early stages of your life, you are not super wealthy, you will slowly but surely grow an asset base that will hold you in good stead later on.

Try to learn the art of flexibility, and don't butt heads with others. You may experience relationship problems if you don't become more accommodating of other people's opinions. Developing listening skills will be one of your main lessons in life. Learning humility is the key to achieving a greater level of harmony in your personal relationships, both social and marital.

Taurus–Gemini Cusp

The tenacity and determination of your typical Taurus Sun sign is given an interesting intellectual twist by having Gemini as an influence on your personality. This means that if you were born in the last week of Taurus—between the 15th and the 22nd of May—you will have a mixture of influences from Taurus as well as Gemini.

The typical Venus influence of your Taurus Sun sign is quickened by the Mercurial Gemini influence. You have a curious nature and can use your imagination in a practical way. Unlike the typical Gemini, who has difficulty in stabilising their thoughts, you are much steadier and have greater command over your thinking processes. You will use these gifts to achieve success in life.

Although you still have the stability and tenacity of your Taurus Sun sign, you're also influenced by the intellectual and curious Gemini. Your communication will be interesting and compassionate at the same time. You have many things to teach others, but have no time for impractical ideas that cannot enhance your life and provide the security you desire for your family and loved ones.

You're never in danger of being too impulsive or outspoken, because you have the ability to put yourself in another person's shoes and think about how they would react. Although you are clever in your speech, you measure your words and are able to make a great impression on others. You give worthwhile advice, and people come to you to receive assistance with their problems. Sharing your wealth of experience helps the community and the world at large.

You don't have difficulty in making a decision, but you like to look at all the alternatives before moving forward. Some people think you're indecisive, but this is not the case. You are careful not only to assess a good outcome, but to see what the downside of the situation might be as well. You cover all bases.

One area you need to be careful of is holding on to your opinions too strongly. Even if you are right on some issues, there may be times when it is better to eat a little humble pie to keep the peace. This is an important lesson to learn, so that you don't become an island unto yourself. Give others the opportunity to express their opinions, remembering to see things from other people's points of view.

TAURUS CELEBRITIES

FAMOUS MALE: GEORGE CLOONEY

George Clooney exudes the most wonderful Venus traits, the trademarks of his Taurus star sign. Charisma, physical attractiveness and extraordinary good luck are the positive attributes of being born under this sign.

George was born in Lexington, Kentucky, and was the son of Nick Clooney, a reasonably successful newscaster at a television station. He hosted a television talk show in Cincinnati. It was in these early years that George was introduced to the world of television, when his father invited him in to learn what it was all about. When George was older, he didn't want to enter into competition with his father, and so gave up his short lived job in broadcast journalism.

George later studied at Northern Kentucky University but had several failures there, including being unsuccessful in joining the Cincinnati Reds baseball team. By a twist of fate, however, his cousin Miguel Ferrer offered him a very small part in a feature film, and this was the beginning of a stellar career for this Taurus film star.

He moved to Los Angeles in 1982 and, in his attempts to make it to the big time of Hollywood, he even slept in his friend's closet. His first movie, with co-star Charlie Sheen, was never released, but it did capture the attention of leading producers who assisted him in acquiring film contracts. The rest is history.

There's an interesting quote from George that sums up his Taurus nature and his ability to make money, come hell or high water. Taurus is one of the most resourceful zodiac signs, and is very economical.

Some people thought he was Tom Cruise's and Nicole Kidman's bodyguard. He remarked that strangers would ask him, 'Is it okay if I go up and ask for an autograph? It was good. I would charge them three dollars a person. Yeah, you gonna make some money off of that!'

Some fantastic opportunities await George during 2012, because Jupiter, the exceptionally beneficial and lucky planet, transits his Sun sign during 2012. This heralds the beginning of an expansive period and one that will be extraordinarily successful for him. He must watch his diet, however, because Jupiter is notorious for holding on to a few kilojoules.

FAMOUS FEMALE: PENÉLOPE CRUZ

The Spanish Enchantress, as she's known outside her native country of Spain, was already an accomplished performer as a toddler, when she re-enacted television commercials for her family. Although she was gifted in the art of acting, she chose to specialise in music and dance.

Once again, we see the powerful energies of Taurus through its ruling planet, Venus, endowing this young lady with the loveliest of talents, and seeing her study classical ballet at nine years of age at Spain's National Conservatory. Unknown to many people, she trained under some very prominent dance tutors until, at the age of fifteen, she was able to audition for a talent agency against 300 other young hopefuls.

One thing you'll note when looking at Penélope is that she has the grace and charm so often associated with people born under the Venusian sign of Taurus. Always elegant, tasteful in attire, and appealing in her looks, Penélope presents the ideal traits of this star sign.

As good fortune would have it, she secured several roles on Spanish television shows and music videos, which of course gave her the opportunity to break into more prominent films. Her first big opportunity came in 1993, and since then she has been a well-known face on screens and televisions across the world, starring with some of the biggest names in Hollywood.

With Venus transiting her career zone in the first month of 2012, this is an excellent omen for her professional life in the coming year. Coupled with the fact that Neptune, which rules photography and film, is also in this star sign, she can expect more success due to their positive positions.

TAURUS
AT LARGE

TELEVISION: A MEDIUM. SO-CALLED BECAUSE IT'S NEITHER RARE NOR WELL DONE.

Ernie Kovacs

TAURUS MAN

TAURUS MAN: SNAPSHOT

Resourceful

Physically strong

Stubborn

Finishes what he starts

Great provider

Taurus men are usually solid and robust-looking individuals, who sometimes tend to be overweight due to their excessive lifestyles. They are usually big-boned and have prominent necks and jaws.

As far as your personality is concerned, you are the plodder of the zodiac, the one who isn't scared to take your time in this day and age of fast-paced, reckless endeavour. There is still something a little old-fashioned about the way you approach your work, your relationships and your day-to-day activities. If someone was to watch you as an impartial spectator, they might even say you are moving in slow motion. Time, to you, is regarded differently to others. You will work slowly and patiently to achieve your prize, and realise that haste does indeed make waste.

You are strongly opinionated but don't always speak up in the first instance. You need to be comfortable with others before voicing your views. But when you feel you have something to say, you don't necessarily choose the conventional fad or point of view, as most do. When pushed, you are as stubborn as the Bull, which is your totem. You dig in your heels and don't budge an inch, especially if challenged on a principle that you hold near and dear.

Many Taurean men like to achieve a high degree of success in their work, and do indeed take their responsibilities very seriously. The reason you are singled out as a great worker by your employers is that you like to do your work exceedingly skilfully, without thought for the time involved. This doesn't win you Brownie points when there are deadlines at stake, but the number one priority in your mind is a job well done.

Although you will be a rather harsh, earthy, and at times insensitive, you do have a sympathetic and compassionate side to your personality, which is most notably seen in your family relationships. You are extremely protective and nurturing of the ones you love. You are an incredibly great provider of all that is needed by your mate and children. In short, family life sits very high on your list of what constitutes a fulfilling life.

Consultation is essential for developing harmony in your personal relationships. Often you feel as if you have all the answers and know exactly how you want to achieve the end result, but if you overlook the needs of your partner, you will create difficulties for your ongoing relationships.

Talk about what you want, and allow others to have a say in the process. It won't always be easy, because you do have a stubborn streak in your nature. Consultation is the one key thing for you to do, to become a better person, and to adapt yourself to your environment and the people in it.

It is a fact that many men born under the sign of Taurus have an innate creative flair. However, because you have the quality of earth as part of your zodiac sign, you probably have a preference for expressing your creative tendencies in a very practical manner. Architecture, landscape design, building, or any other hands-on project that requires your artistic input is the perfect way to explore this Taurean ability.

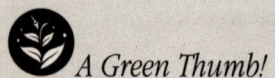

A Green Thumb!

Speaking of earth, I have found many Taureans love to garden and get their hands dirty in the soil. Many have a green thumb and are able to produce lovely gardens which, once in bloom, give them a wonderful sense of peace and happiness. This especially applies to men born under the sign of the Bull.

It's interesting to note that the sign of the zodiac relating to your personal development is the progressive sign of Aquarius. This is one of the main challenges for you, Taurus, to progress and excel beyond your own personal limitations. This sign indicates that it is necessary for you to transcend the limitations you have placed on yourself in a harmonious way. Enjoy the moment and live life to the fullest.

TAURUS WOMAN

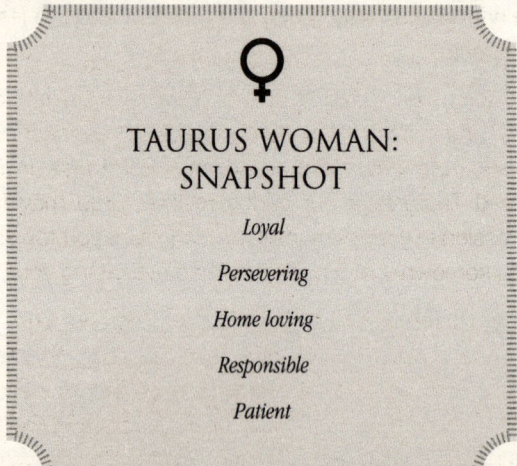

TAURUS WOMAN: SNAPSHOT

Loyal

Persevering

Home loving

Responsible

Patient

A delicate balance of grace and strength best describes women born under the sign of Taurus. I find it ironic that the soft and gentle planet Venus is represented by the horned Bull. When people first meet you, they see only the softer, quieter and less demanding side of your personality. Once you reveal the part of your character that is more determined, people will understand that you have many different colours to your nature.

You are a persevering, determined and loving person. However, there are a few things that bother you, some of which turn you from Dr Jekyll into Mr Hyde, and these should be noted. First and foremost is the element of honesty, which rests upon loyalty. To you, loyalty is everything. If anyone would like to see the dominant, aggressive and bull-like nature that is often talked about when referring to Taurus, they simply need to deceive you or break your trust. It's at this point that your bullish side will come charging out.

Being an earth sign means you are grounded and never look down your nose at others. You never forget your roots, and for this reason you're able to connect with anyone from any class of society. For those more-evolved Taureans, your earthy relative Virgo may find expression in your personality, which leads you towards being somewhat of a perfectionist in everything you do.

I have personally met many Taurean women who are very houseproud. Their home is their castle and they tend to its every detail, making excellent hostesses when anyone comes to visit. They understand the art of nurturing, loving and providing comfort to others, not just to their own kids—any stranger who needs a hand will always be well looked after by them.

Because you have a particular way of doing things, you may be regarded as critical of others, preferring everyone do things your way. You must learn to be more flexible, especially with your children, who often find your demands for perfection too hard to bear. Actually, you always have other people's best interests at heart, and it is simply how you deliver your caring ways that may need some slight modification.

You also exhibit this trait in the way you work. This applies equally to your co-workers and employers. Nevertheless, no one can fault that you are sincere, persevering and diligent in executing your responsibilities.

Even if you don't have a lot of money, you have an inbuilt sense of economy and can stretch a dollar a great distance. As long as you don't let the excessive side of Venus dominate your desire for sensual excess, you'll be able to harmonise these needs with the practical realities of life.

In relationships, you don't like arguments and will avoid any head-on collisions, so to speak. You prefer to walk away gracefully, but this too has its downside. You'll eventually appreciate that you need to address issues rather than bottle them up. The sooner you deal with problems, the sooner you'll be able to become the woman you were potentially born to be.

Taurean women make some of the best mothers in the zodiac. You are protective, loving and supportive of your children, and will do anything to give them the best in life. However, you must remember not to ignore your partner, because sometimes you become fixated on the needs of your children.

TAURUS CHILD

Being an expert psychologist wouldn't be a bad idea if your child happens to be born under the sign of Taurus—you will need to be clever in dealing with their stubborn nature. Following your rules and regulations is not exactly going to be their forte, so showing them how to do things and getting them to toe the line will be one of your biggest challenges as a parent.

From the word go, you will need to understand their tendency to take shortcuts, cut corners, and their preference for ease and comfort. Your responsibility as a parent is to stimulate them, and to give them a sense of achievement, a schedule to live by and a strong code of discipline, through which they can develop themselves.

Cuddly Taurus

Children of a Taurus are loving because they are born under the sensual rays of Venus. As such, emotional attention, nurturing and cuddling will be food for their souls. If you give them love, they will immediately respond in-kind and show their loving ways to you.

You must not lock them away from their social group: they need companions and enjoy the company of friends. They are particularly sociable and like to combine their creativity with their relationships. However, you must be careful to monitor their sexual interests and activities as they get older.

I mentioned earlier the tendency towards sluggishness for Taurus, which can be overcome through exercise and sport. You need to mobilise your Taurean child and give them ample opportunity to breathe fresh air, bathe in the sunshine and move their bodies in a healthy environment.

Some of the less-evolved children of this star sign tend to be bullies— excuse the pun—so again, it is your responsibility to make sure they respect others and don't always get their own way. This may be more apparent if they are an only child and have not learned the art of sharing. It is easy to spoil them, and their selfishness will be a problem if it becomes a habit, especially once they are at school and in the company of others. Harmonious relationships are always a matter of give and take. Teach this important life lesson to them.

Taurean children are loving, supportive and adore being part of a family. They are loyal and can be trusted to complete a task. You should set them chores from an early age so that being active becomes an ingrained habit. Keeping them busy will prevent laziness and sloth becoming permanent parts of their characters.

TAURUS LOVER

❝ DON'T LET SOMEONE BE A PRIORITY IN YOUR LIFE WHEN YOU ARE STILL AN OPTION IN THEIRS. (UNKNOWN) ❞

You are one of the most loyal and dedicated of the zodiac signs and stability is highly prized by you when it comes to relationships. In reading this, Taurus, you'll understand what I mean when I say, the sensual and sexual side of your life takes a back seat to stability, both financially and emotionally. Unless you feel comfortable and at ease with the person you are with, then you find it hard to let go, open up and give your heart completely to them.

You have a tendency to get stuck following certain patterns in life, and relationships are no exception. This could also apply to situations where you've broken up with someone, and once that happens, it's not easy for you to let go of the romance you may have given everything to. Allowing time for you to heal could be a long and drawn-out process, until you're ready to attempt love again, if ever. You do, however, need a partner by your side, so you must always remain open to the possibilities that life can bring you.

In love, you are possessive, just as you are with some of your material belongings. And if you choose someone with whom you want to spend your life, they must be 100 per cent committed to the cause. You mustn't, however, allow jealousy to take hold of you, especially if these feelings and negative attitudes are baseless. You must, under all circumstances, extend trust and a sense of independence to the one you love. By doing so, you'll find that your partner will reciprocate and be less prone to wandering. Trying to smother your lover would be disastrous to your relationship.

You prefer to fall in love with someone who is financially stable. This doesn't mean that he or she needs to be a multimillionaire, though. To you it's enough if the person has a regular, steady income, a good pattern of saving, and responsible economic views.

Although you are honest, sometimes you are quite simple and straightforward in the way you approach things. I might add that some people might find you a little too honest. Good communication may sometimes require you to explain yourself, and go into the reasoning behind what you've said in a bit more depth. Try to develop this component of your relationships, because there may be occasions where you can't express yourself any further and move you into shutdown mode, to the detriment of what could otherwise be a great relationship.

With adaptability comes a better opportunity for compromise, which is also absolutely necessary for relationships to thrive. You should try your hardest to remain open to doing things a little differently, to being a little more spontaneous for your partner, and enjoying life without worrying too much about money. Being frugal and security conscious is important, but not at the expense of the development of a relationship with someone who may like some excitement and spontaneity from time to time.

Once the sensual elements of your nature come to the surface, you tend to become fixated on the pleasurable aspects of the feelings that arise from them. Try not to allow yourself to get carried away by overindulging in the sensate parts of your personality. Once again, the secret—as with anything, but particularly in your relationships—is moderation.

No Fly-by-Nighters

When you do finally meet someone you are attracted to, Taurus, you need quite a bit of warm-up time to get to know them, to see if they're serious and whether or not you can make a life with them. As I've said before, for you, love is for keeps, particularly if you're in your 30s or older. You're not that interested in fly-by-night romances or one-night stands.

TAURUS FRIEND

You don't like to get too close to people too quickly. You actually pride yourself on the fact that you can count the number of your truly close friends on one hand. You are a good friend and enjoy meeting new people, but not simply for the sake of it. You shun superficiality and egotism of any sort. Perhaps for this reason you attract only genuine people who will return your trust and loyalty.

Once you make a friend, you like to hang on to that person, to develop trust and a depth of connection with them over a period of time. You're certainly not the type of person to spill the beans on the first date or first meeting, but prefer to savour tidbits of information, putting together the jigsaw of who that person is over time. In this manner, you can slowly digest the many different facets of a friend's personality, history and connections with you.

You love to entertain, to wine and dine, and therefore friendship for you is a social occasion that has as much to do with the lunch or dinner and good wine as it does your companion. You find sharing this activity to be a bridge between your mind and theirs. You love to enjoy different foods from various cultures and places, and discovering new restaurants is something that will bring you closer to any friend who shares this pastime.

You probably have a birthday book, Taurus—and you might chuckle while I'm saying this—but I know you're not the type to forget a special date, birthday or event, and people who consider you a friend really appreciate this. Not only that, but when it comes to purchasing a gift for someone you love, you spend a lot of time considering what it is that would make them feel happy. I've even seen Taureans go to the trouble of making something very unique and personal because they have great handicraft skills.

You're extremely dependable, and friends look to you for guidance and stability. Even in times of trouble, you seem to be rather anchored, stable and earthy in your approach to problems, and aren't swayed by the passing trends and fads of life. This makes you an excellent advisor to others in times of need, which goes hand in glove with being a good friend. When people need your advice, you are there to give them a practical assessment of the situation, without any embellishment or bias on your part.

For others, having a Taurus as their friend is a deep and committed exercise. Don't expect Taureans to take their friendships lightly. If they are loyal and devoted to you, you'll have to give as good as you take.

TAURUS ENEMY

> **IT IS DIFFICULT TO SAY WHO DO YOU THE MOST HARM: ENEMIES WITH THE WORST INTENTIONS, OR FRIENDS WITH THE BEST. (EDWARD G. BULWER-LYTTON)**

Taurus is rather patient, and averse to any sort of disagreements, especially confrontations. But don't take this to mean they won't stand up and fight, particularly if they've been wronged by someone and consider them an enemy.

Generally, as an enemy, Taureans are able to keep their grudges under wraps, and you may not even know what's bothering them. But take note that the Bull can only suppress his or her feelings for so long, and then an explosion is imminent. It's not a matter of *if* they will charge, but *when*.

Although it takes a considerable amount of push and shove to rile them, Taurus does have a dark side. Being ruled by the Bull means they can make a mess of things when their horns get stuck into you, and they will damage those things or people who have crossed them. Also, because Taurus is possessive with their belongings and even more so with the people they love, any wrongdoing in the department of love is likely to arouse their jealousy or, worse still, their anger.

In personal circumstances where they have been wronged, and you are the friend that has done something they feel is unforgivable, you will see the furious and sometimes aggressive side of Taurus come to the fore. You'll be left asking yourself: 'Where did this violent avalanche of anger and power come from, in one normally so meek and mild?'

Just remember, Taurus never forgets an insult or wrongdoing, and it could be years, if ever, before they forgive someone they deem to be an enemy.

TAURUS
AT HOME

DO WHATEVER IT TAKES TO CONVEY
YOUR ESSENTIAL SELF.

Martha Beck

HOME FRONT

The driving force behind the Taurus personality is security. Because you want to feel safe and secure, having a warm and comfortable home is an important component of your overall wellbeing and satisfaction in life. In particular, having a family around you plays a key role in your experience of an even greater degree of security and happiness. Your home truly is your sanctuary.

In your home environment, you like a soft and relaxed atmosphere where you can wind down and enjoy the company of your family or, at times, just your own company. Being an earth sign, having a lovely garden with fragrant flowers to accent your interior design is usually part and parcel of the Taurean lifestyle.

Having a sunny porch or sunroom where you can just laze about with a coffee, cookies and your favourite book on a Sunday afternoon, with the sweet smell of roses wafting in, is something you probably dream of. Oh, I probably forgot the white picket fence!

You'll find many a Taurus in the kitchen, because you love to cook and, of course, to eat! Fresh, earthy ingredients, including herbs, and even vegetables you've grown yourself, will be found in your kitchen. Cooking for your loved ones is the ideal way to express your Taurus pride and the fact that you value your home and family life so much.

Luxurious Taurus

You like soft fabrics, elegant curtains and carpets. Luxurious comfort is sure to be an important feature of your decorating ideas. Interestingly, because many of you are rather economical with your money, you can make your house look a lot more expensive than it really is.

Creating space is essential for you, especially if you lead a hectic life from Monday to Friday. You need time on your own in a sacred space that is privately yours, where no one else can bother you. It should be a room in which you can revitalise yourself, feel cosy and comfortable, and reconnect with private things: your inner self that is yours and yours alone.

Taureans are very houseproud and like showing off their places of residence extravagantly. Keeping up with the Joneses may, for some of you born under this sign, become a problem. As far as furnishings are concerned, you don't like things to be too outlandish, although you like to have some traditional or ornate things with a luxurious feel to them. In any case, as long as your home is clean and everything is placed in the same spot it usually is, you'll feel happy. One of your pet gripes is people moving furniture around just when you've become used to the layout.

Touch, the feel of the furniture, and the colour scheme are all important. You love pastels and colours that are not too hard on the eye. Soft curves and gentle lighting also express your Taurean temperament wonderfully.

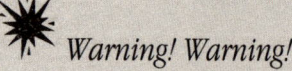 *Warning! Warning!*

Never move a piece of furniture without asking a Taurus. They hate their interior decor being messed with!

KARMA, LUCK AND MEDITATION

Taurus usually earns their luck through their slow, steady and patient action in life. Luck may not always occur suddenly or quickly. You mustn't rely on others for your success, but on your own efforts and intuition. Even if what is offered to you seems like a gift on a silver platter, you just don't trust success that comes that easily.

Saturn rules your zone of past karma and good fortune. Because of this, you may need to wait till later in life to harvest your karmic fruits. The good luck you receive will sometimes be the result of the extra hard effort you put in, and possibly of the challenges and obstacles that others don't experience. Such is the influence of Saturn on your life.

Future Karma

Your future karma, and what is likely to happen in your life, are ruled by Virgo and Mercury. Mercury is a lucky planet, which indicates a bright future if you communicate openly and don't bottle up your emotions. Work with these principles and with this planet to free up its lucky vibrations: they will come back to you in the form of success, wealth and good relationships.

'I Possess' is your life phrase. Try to become more aware of your self—that is, who you are—as distinct from what you own. Your possessions are not the most important measure of who you are. Once you realise this, you will enjoy what you have all the more, because you will experience another dimension to your being: a spiritual one. This is the best way for Taurus to find peace of mind and to achieve superior happiness.

Wednesdays, Fridays and Saturdays are lucky for emotional healing and self-development. Spend a little time each day doing something spontaneous that you wouldn't normally do—this will augment your luck.

Lucky Days
Your luckiest days are Wednesday, Friday and Saturday.

Lucky Numbers
Lucky numbers for Taurus include the following. You may wish to experiment with these in lotteries and other games of chance:

6, 15, 24, 33, 42, 51

5, 14, 23, 32, 41, 50

8, 17, 26, 35, 44, 53

Destiny Years
The most significant years in your life are likely to be 6, 15, 24, 33, 42, 51, 60, 78 and 87.

HEALTH, WELLBEING AND DIET

You are lucky to be born under Taurus when it comes to discussions about health, but not so lucky with regards to diet. Of course, the two go hand in glove. I say lucky in the first instance because you are naturally born with a resilient nature and, usually, a solidly built physique, which can withstand extremes in climate and environment, and you are being endowed with indomitable stamina.

I say not so lucky in the second instance because you have a tendency towards excess. It is now a well-known fact that you can't really separate good health from what you eat. So the first and foremost requirement for a Taurean, to ensure your good health, is to apply moderation in eating, drinking and living patterns.

Your constitution will be so much stronger if you pay attention to your body signals and the responses you receive after eating certain types of foods. As an example, Taurus, being ruled by Venus, has a sweet tooth. You love anything sweet, rich and luscious, anything fully textured and with a variety of flavours. As a consequence, you may end up mixing too many food types together, which is not at all in keeping with what your digestive system can manage. By *listening* to your body, you will soon know the effects of this mish-mash of culinary delights on your physical wellbeing.

Avoid an excess of sugar, candy, cakes and other fattening foods. Eat lean, white meat in preference to heavy, fatty, red meat and other animal products. This will give you an immense lift in your energy levels.

Taurus rules the throat, mouth, neck and face. These parts of your body may cause you health troubles at some point in life. Your tonsils, thyroid and parathyroid should be checked every so often.

FINANCE FINESSE

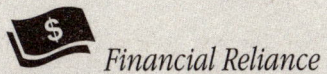

Financial Reliance

For Taurus, money signifies a very deep and emotional issue in life. To them it is a measure of security and their ability to remain happy and contented. Without money Taurus doesn't function well. Life loses its pleasure, and worry and apprehension take over very easily.

Taurus is an earth sign and the natural ruler of the financial area of the zodiac. It indicates money, material resources and things of value in this world. This is why Taureans, from an early age, place great emphasis on finding a way of earning money that will give them both creature comforts and a secure future path, which they instinctively feel is important to them.

Sometimes the importance of money can take on abnormal proportions and get in the road of otherwise well-functioning and harmonious relationships. You must be careful to balance your need to earn against those emotional and relationship needs that are more subtle in nature. Try not to overemphasise the importance of money, possessions and other outward displays, which are in the end, only accessories to real happiness.

TAURUS
AT WORK

IT'S A RARE THING TO FIND
SOMEBODY YOU CAN WORK WITH,
WORK OFF OF, AND HAVE FUN WITH.

Matthew Ashford

TAURUS CAREER

IDEAL PROFESSIONS

Events production

Real estate

Building design and construction

Landscape architecture

Interior design

Finance, banking and investment

Taureans are well suited to practical jobs. Without the steady foundational support of Taurus in the workplace, it's quite likely a business could fall to pieces. Slow, steady and plodding best describe Taureans engaged in any sort of work, however menial or stimulating. Taurus is disciplined and capable of following through on a task with diligence and a sense of responsibility. This is exactly what a business needs to succeed.

The excellent work ethic of Taurus is highly respected by co-workers and employers. Taureans take pride in their work, and you will know what I mean by this, Taurus, even if your work is that of a homemaker or domestic help. You always endeavour to put a touch of perfection on whatever you do, treating your work as an expression of love and nurturing.

However, in any workplace scenario that has high tension, deadlines or commitments forcing you to work beyond your comfort level, you may find it difficult keeping up with those who call the shots. For those of you reading this who have to deal with a Taurus as a co-worker or an employee, you need to be mindful of the fact that they work better without too much stress, at their own pace and on their own terms.

Perhaps a compromise may need to be reached if a faster pace is required of a Taurus worker. Rest assured, however, that the end result will be very satisfying if Taureans are left to their own devices, because they like to dot their i's and cross their t's rather than make errors. They hate to make mistakes, and have a strong sense of pride in their work.

Venus

Your workplace planet is Venus, Taurus. What does this mean to you professionally? Because Venus has much to do with beauty, fashion, the arts, film, dance and other creative areas, anything along these lines is a great professional path for you. Let's not forget to mention that Taurus also does well in professions relating to gardening, horticulture and home crafts.

Uranus

Once you let go of your traditional modes of thinking, the planet Uranus, your career planet, will give you the strength and open-mindedness to attempt something progressive and unique. Strangely, modern technological businesses and careers can suit some Taureans.

TAURUS BOSS

When working for a Taurus boss, employees will have to get used to the fact that things are to be done their way. In an office environment, the Taurus boss is an imposing figure who is usually quite conservative and controlled in his or her emotions. They need to have a straightforward, peaceful and well-ordered environment to function comfortably in their role as administrator. They like a homely and comfortable—if not palatial—type of environment in which to function professionally. If these are the sorts of qualities you admire in your employer, then you should get on quite well with your Taurean boss.

Taurus employers are very persevering and patient, and also somewhat finicky about the way they like things done. They are always slow and methodical in coming to a conclusion. If your timelines are out of sync with your boss, you could have a problem. Be warned: there's no rushing your Taurean boss to meet your expectations! You'll be left waiting until they've made up their mind, which can sometimes be a challenge for employees.

Every aspect of their day-to-day business life runs like clockwork. They prefer to have a well-ordered schedule and expect everyone to stick to it. They hate surprises, and if there is the odd time when you need to take a little time out, you're warned to give adequate notice or see that bull-like anger come to the surface. This doesn't often happen, but when Taurean anger rears its ugly head, employees should take cover!

Taurean bosses are stubborn but, by the same token, they're very loyal to their employees and support them in any way they can, particularly if their employees have, over a period of time, also exhibited considerable loyalty to them. They are devoted to their spouse as much as they are to their business, and they understand that a good working relationship is going to help them achieve their goals.

TAURUS EMPLOYEE

As an employer, you can't go past a Taurus as a steadfast and reliable worker, who will do their very best in the job allocated to them. You must, however, understand a few things about your Taurus employee if you are to gain the maximum benefit from them.

Financial Reliance

The first and foremost thing to bear in mind is that Taurean employees need a well-ordered and structured schedule in which to perform. The other thing is that they are particularly keen on completing their tasks well, and if this means taking extra time to do so, then continually pushing them to meet a deadline could become a problem for you.

You'll learn that Taureans sometimes avoid confrontation, and even though they may be particularly angry at something you've said or done, or that they feel is unfair, they'll rarely speak up unless asked to give an opinion. When they are asked, you can expect an honest but low-key answer.

Because Taureans very much like to create comfortable, relaxed and homely surroundings, you can expect your Taurean employee to add a touch of flair to what might otherwise be a bland and inhospitable environment known as the office. Taurus will create mood by strategically placing a bunch of flowers in the waiting room or lobby, adding a nice, colourful painting in the hallway, and generally redesigning and decorating the office to make it more friendly and inviting.

Because Taurus individuals hate change, it's not likely (if you provide them with a fair salary and good working conditions) that they will desert you. They are known for dependability, punctuality and a work ethic that is second to none. You must, however, never put them in a position where they have to compromise their ethics, or place them under stress because of any inefficiencies, chaotic routines or instability arising from your own poor management. This won't be tolerated too well by Taurus.

RESPECTFUL TAURUS

Once they commit themselves to a job, even if they don't particularly like you as their employer, they will show due deference and respect to you for being in the position of authority.

PROFESSIONAL RELATIONSHIPS: BEST AND WORST

BEST PAIRING: TAURUS AND CAPRICORN

You have a special affinity with the zodiac sign of Capricorn, not just on a personal level, but professionally and financially. The significant elemental similarity of earth underpins this special relationship, which will produce extraordinary results for the two of you in any business situation.

As a Taurus, you know without me telling you that money, security and working in a job that can give you creative satisfaction are some of the most important ingredients in your life. If these components are not present, you become pretty miserable. This is where Capricorn comes in: offering you much of what you seek in the work sphere of your life.

Capricorn, like you, is not overly concerned with achieving results quickly. Rather, they have a conservative approach and like to do things with a long-term view in mind. They don't tend to worry too much if everyone around them is achieving things at a faster pace, as long as they keep their mind focused on their ambitions and reach their goals on their own terms.

In a similar fashion, you like to work in a way that is in keeping with your personality, and this means taking your time, doing things well and showing pride in your finished work. It doesn't matter whether Capricorn is your employer or employee, there will always be mutual respect because of this shared attribute. Capricorn understands your spin on things. Your Capricorn business partner will give you the scope to do things at the pace you need because they are pretty much in tune with your timeline.

Capricorn is practical and financially savvy, just as you are. Neither of you are lavish spenders until you feel you have the financial security to justify purchasing luxury items. You are similarly minded in terms of self-sacrificing for your business, or until your financial position is so strong, that you can reward yourself for a job well done by buying the best.

Capricorn is ruled by Saturn, a planet that also has an affinity with the revolutionary sign of Aquarius. Simply put, Capricorn having Aquarius as the sign of finance reveals that they are very shrewd. They are ingenious in coming up with moneymaking schemes and acquiring lots of money through their hard work. You admire these traits.

WORST PAIRING: TAURUS AND AQUARIUS

Aquarius and Taurus are diametrically opposed on different levels due to the ruling planets of your respective signs. You are ruled by Venus, which is a more conservative planet than Uranus, the ruler of Aquarius. Aquarius needs to go beyond the limits of convention, challenging traditional methods and institutions and discovering breathtakingly new methodologies in work, society and even their personal sphere. From your initial contact with Aquarius, you will feel uneasy, challenged and worried.

Aquarius may have some concerns about money, but not in the way you do. They're prepared to take risks—sometimes uncalculated ones— which are based on their hugely unconventional vision of life and its possibilities. Sadly, you, Taurus, don't have the same confidence and prefer to stick with what has been tried and tested. On this principle alone, I can predict the two of you will have many confrontational episodes, each of you trying to gain the upper hand in convincing the other that you are right.

Apart from the issue of money, you may also feel somewhat uncomfortable working with each other because you fear the courageous attitude of your Aquarian partner. You are not necessarily respectful of each other's views, and will slowly find out that you are unable to contribute to what the other has to say. You generally disagree over the direction that your business or creative ideals should take.

There are some obvious differences between you and Aquarius, but the funny thing is, this is related to the similar fixity of your star signs. This means neither of you is able to adjust yourself to the other's needs, nor to the circumstances you find yourselves in commercially.

TAURUS
IN LOVE

WE WERE GIVEN: TWO HANDS TO HOLD. TWO LEGS TO WALK. TWO EYES TO SEE. TWO EARS TO LISTEN. BUT WHY ONLY ONE HEART? BECAUSE THE SECOND WAS GIVEN TO SOMEONE ELSE, FOR US TO FIND.

Unknown

ROMANTIC COMPATIBILITY

How compatible are you with your current partner, lover or friend? Did you know that astrology can reveal a whole new level of understanding between people, simply by looking at their star sign and that of their partner? I'd like to share some special insights that will help you better appreciate your strengths and challenges using Sun sign compatibility.

The Sun reflects your drive, willpower and personality. The essential qualities of two star signs blend like two pure colours that produce an entirely new colour. Relationships, similarly, produce their own emotional colours when two people interact. The following section is a general guide to your romantic prospects with others and how, by knowing the astrological 'colour' of each other, the art of love can help you create a masterpiece.

Each of the twelve star signs has a greater or lesser affinity with the others. The two quick-reference tables will show you who's hot and who's not as far as your relationships are concerned.

The Star Sign Compatibility table rates your chance as a percentage of general compatibility, while the Horoscope Compatibility table summarises the reasons why. The results of each star sign combination are also listed.

When reading I ask you to remember that no two star signs are ever *totally* incompatible. With effort and compromise, even the most difficult astrological matches can work. Don't close your mind to the full range of life's possibilities! Learning about each other and ourselves is the most important facet of astrology.

Good luck in your search for love, and may the stars shine upon you in 2012!

STAR SIGN COMPATIBILITY FOR LOVE AND FRIENDSHIP (PERCENTAGES)

	Aries	Taurus	Gemini	Cancer	Leo	Virgo	Libra	Scorpio	Sagittarius	Capricorn	Aquarius	Pisces
Aries	60	65	65	65	90	45	70	80	90	50	55	65
Taurus	60	70	70	80	70	90	75	85	50	95	80	85
Gemini	70	70	75	60	80	75	90	60	75	50	90	50
Cancer	65	80	60	75	70	75	60	95	55	45	70	90
Leo	90	70	80	70	85	75	65	75	95	45	70	75
Virgo	45	90	75	75	75	70	80	85	70	95	50	70
Libra	70	75	90	60	65	80	80	85	80	85	95	50
Scorpio	80	85	60	95	75	85	85	90	80	65	60	95
Sagittarius	90	50	75	55	95	70	80	85	85	55	60	75
Capricorn	50	95	50	45	45	95	85	65	55	85	70	85
Aquarius	55	80	90	70	70	50	95	60	60	70	80	55
Pisces	65	85	50	90	75	70	50	95	75	85	55	80

In the compatibility table above please note that some compatibilities have seemingly contradictory ratings. Why you ask? Well, remember that no two people experience the relationship in exactly the same way. For one person a relationship may be more advantageous, more supportive than for the other. Sometimes one gains more than the other partner and therefore the compatibility rating will be higher for them.

HOROSCOPE COMPATIBILITY FOR TAURUS

Taurus with		Romance/Sexual
Aries		Loving and passionate affair, turbulent at times
Taurus		Loving and sensual match: star twins
Gemini		Great friends and lovers, with Gemini stimulating Taurus
Cancer		Moody Cancer is anchored by your steady love
Leo		Exciting in the bedroom, but both of you have fixed ways

	Friendship		Professional
✔	Good friends, but Aries tries to dominate	✔	Good combination: Aries is the engine and Taurus is the chassis
✔	Common interests, but could stagnate without initiative	✔	Good financial match
✔	Interesting communication but Gemini needs more intellectual stimulation	✔	Creative match that fuels both of your ambitions
✘	Cancer is way too sensitive for you—take control of them	✔	Cancer gains considerably through this match
✔	Can stimulate each other; Lions can eat bulls, however, so don't provoke Leo	✔	Strong connection that can bring success

Taurus with		Romance/Sexual
Virgo		One of the great combinations of the zodiac; romance can blossom
Libra		Common sexual and intimate interests, but Libra may be too flighty for you
Scorpio		Strong attraction and likely to last, but punctuated by extreme ups and downs
Sagittarius		Complete mismatch: you will frustrate each other
Capricorn		The Goat makes you feel sexually secure, and moves at a similar pace; you turn them on
Aquarius		Progressive Aquarius is too unconventional and unpredictable, and you don't understand their ways

	Friendship		Professional
✓	Good pals, but Taurus doesn't appreciate Virgo's fault-finding nature	✓	Good speculative match, balanced by Taurus's caution and economy
✓	Libra is a good friend yet needs room to socialise—don't be possessive with them	✓	Libra provides fresh ideas—take them on board and don't get stuck in the past
✓	Generally good friends, but Scorpio demands a lot of attention	✗	Too stubborn to concede that the other may be able to show you something new
✓	Warm, exciting match; an adventurous combination	✗	Taurus serves Sagittarius well, but not the other way around
✓	Conventional Capricorn is your cup of tea, socially speaking— you have common interests	✓	Great teamwork between you, much can be achieved—a successful partnership
✓	Aquarius stimulates Taurus and makes you step outside the square	✓	Ingenious Aquarius can help you forge a new career path

Taurus with	Romance/Sexual
Pisces	Pisces will love Taurus unconditionally, however, Pisces is too idealistic

Friendship	Professional
✔ Initially a good friendship, but can run into snags philosophically	✔ Pisces offers you good financial options

TAURUS PARTNERSHIPS

Taurus + Aries

Aries stimulates you, while you anchor them and provide some solid stability in their lives. You're practical and, with your security conscious attitude, will give Aries firm, gentle guidance. Power and control will be areas you need to deal with. You are good together sexually.

Taurus + Taurus

In each other you find direction—or that need for security—and have the ability to fulfil each other. Money, a comfortable house and a good family life will be common interests. The only danger is that you may both be too complacent and become couch potatoes.

Taurus + Gemini

Gemini stimulates your imagination which is useful for you to develop your personality. Sexually, you feel comfortable with each other, because your ruling planets are very friendly. You'll be attracted to Gemini's curious and inventive mind. They love your sensuality while you adore their wit.

Taurus + Cancer

Taurus and Cancer are very compatible astrologically, due to the sensitivity you show each other. Both of you have feminine traits, indicating a loving, compassionate nature. You share the common goals of having a comfortable family life with long-term financial security. Sexual affection is satisfying to you.

Taurus + Leo

You have a very powerful sexual connection with Leo, but be sure to take things slow and easy. Create a little time for the two of you to deepen your affection beyond the superficial. Once that happens, you may be able to have a lasting relationship. You are both quite stubborn in your opinions.

Taurus + Virgo

The two of you make excellent mates because of your common earth element. Most signs react terribly to the critical mind of Virgo, but you, above all the others, can handle Virgo perfectly. Great attraction and a meeting of the minds make this a win-win combination. Lovemaking should also be stimulating for both of you.

Taurus + Libra

Although you're born under the same planetary rulership, there are differences in your styles. Libra needs a little more stimulation than you are prepared to give, at least at the beginning of the relationship. You can work well together if you develop good communication early on.

Taurus + Scorpio

Opposites usually attract, and this is the case with Taurus and Scorpio. However, you are both extremely inflexible in your opinions, and this means the relationship is likely to come unstuck at some point. There is great physical attraction between you, but you also have your differences, both mentally and emotionally.

Taurus + Sagittarius

Sagittarius is way too free and easy for your structured ways. You are concerned about their inability to stay grounded at times. You may not be quite the right type of communicator, and your ruling planets don't exactly feel comfortable with each other. This is not, for the most part, a good match.

Taurus + Capricorn

Once again, the combination of earth signs, to which you both belong, makes this an excellent match. As a couple, you will get on well and have similar objectives in life. This is a stable relationship and one in which you feel mutually supported. Sexually, you are like-minded, with Capricorn being rather traditional in their ways.

Taurus + Aquarius

You are challenged by the progressive ways of Aquarius, so this may not be the best of relationships. If you are open enough to some of their opinions and lifestyle choices, then your friendship could be an interesting journey for you. They are sexually unconventional, which may also be interesting, if only for a while.

Taurus + Pisces

This is a very loving relationship and can be classed as one of the better combinations of the zodiac. Your mutual affection and empathy for each other is great. Pisces supports you 100 per cent in every way. In the bedroom, you have an affinity for each other, which makes this a great partnership.

PLATONIC RELATIONSHIPS: BEST AND WORST

BEST PAIRING: TAURUS AND PISCES

Your initial reaction to being told that Pisces is probably one of your best platonic matches might be one of surprise. Yet Pisces is the eleventh sign to Taurus, indicating a close friendship and lots of social activity. The fact that you are a very practical and down-to-earth person and Pisces is altogether your diametric opposite (that is, spiritual, non-materialistic and sometimes ungrounded), might make this seem an unlikely match, but the two of you balance each other in unusual ways.

This combination is a very good one in astrological terms. You are both capable of building a trusting relationship based upon mutual understanding. And even though Pisces is quite sensitive and moody, you have the ability to connect with the feminine aspect of their temperament, whether they are male or female. The mutable (or adaptable) aspect of the Pisces character is also well suited to you, in that they can handle your somewhat stubborn nature without taking it too hard. You, on the other hand, can teach them the art of being a little firmer in their opinions, and here again we see your capacity to harmonise each other's personalities in a wonderfully unique way.

One important lesson your Piscean friend can learn from you is the art of being more practical with money, and life in general. Some Pisceans have lost their way and, karmically speaking, you have come together to teach each other some important lessons. Conversely, Pisces has the ability to take you away from your material concerns and preoccupation with security, to understand yourself better and gain a deeper insight into the spiritual dynamics of life. And they can do this in a way that doesn't threaten you. Because of this, you accept what they say, observing that they exhibit their spirituality in the way they live from day to day. The Piscean individual certainly arouses your curiosity, that's for sure.

You're able to inspire more self-confidence in your Piscean friend, and they will appreciate this by reciprocating with their support for you. They are not necessarily the type to steal the limelight, and can support you by serving your particular needs without demanding much back from you. The only thing you should be mindful of is never taking advantage of their extraordinarily unconditional love. Once you hurt them, they may never recover. You don't want to lose a friend as good as this.

WORST PAIRING: TAURUS AND LEO

You're both extremely fixed in your personalities and this is why any relationship, and in particular a platonic one, maybe exceedingly challenging between Taurus and Leo. This is not to say there isn't a natural attraction between you, even though your ruling planets don't sit particularly well together in the scheme of the zodiac. Nevertheless, you can experience a great deal of happiness and light-heartedness in the company of each other and in social circumstances.

Your first meeting with a Leo will trigger good feelings because they are ruled by the Sun, which is bright and warm. This naturally draws you to them, and over and above this, they have a great sense of humour and a relaxed and outgoing manner. In some ways you feel a little envious of just how unconcerned they are about other people's opinions.

Taurus is, of course, ruled by Venus, so also has a very sociable and easygoing manner. However, you may not feel quite as relaxed within yourself as Leo does, and you could take on board some of these Leo mannerisms to create greater confidence in yourself. You will most definitely appreciate this.

TAURUS AND LEO MAY NEVER AGREE

Both Taurus and Leo happen to be fixed, immoveable signs of the zodiac, indicating two absolutely inflexible natures. Trying to get each other to agree on a point of difference will always be an impossible task.

Although your initial admiration for Leo is genuine, it may soon wear thin, because they continually seek attention to such an extent that you wonder if, in fact, they have deep insecurities rather than the supreme confidence you may at first have attributed to them.

SEXUAL RELATIONSHIPS: BEST AND WORST

BEST PAIRING: TAURUS AND VIRGO

Ideally, there are three important components in making star signs compatible.

The first is the elemental composition of each star sign. If they are the same, as is the case with Taurus and Virgo, then this goes a long way towards ensuring compatibility, stability and fulfilment in the relationship. In your case, both Taurus and Virgo are classed as earth signs.

The second component has to do with the friendship of the planets that rule you. Taurus is ruled by Venus and Virgo by Mercury, and these two are very friendly in the astrological scheme. This augments the potential for a successful sexual relationship between you.

The third component has to do with the juxtaposition or distance between one star sign and the other. Virgo falls in the fifth zone to your Sun sign. The fifth zone is all about romance, love affairs, creativity and children. This is an added bonus because it shows that you are naturally attracted to each other in a romantic and sexual sense as well.

Based on these three criteria, I have determined your star signs as being ideally compatible sexually.

Because Virgo mirrors some of your personality traits, such as cleanliness, practicality and a sense of service, you find in them much of yourself, and can relate to them very easily. Virgo feels the same about you. So from the very outset, the two of you have a sense of similarity and mutual respect.

It is very important to enjoy the sexual element of a relationship. If you feel uncomfortable with parts of a person's personality, it won't be that easy to open your heart to them in the bedroom. What you love about your Virgo partner is the fact that they are not afraid to humble themselves and serve you in whatever way they can to satisfy your each and every need. That is unusual these days, isn't it, Taurus?

Virgo is prone to being critical, but they see that you are indeed careful in executing any work you choose to take on, so there's not much they can fault in the way you conduct yourself. However, if they do start to pick you to pieces, you are slow to temper, and don't react quite as quickly or vehemently as some of the other star signs. This can obviously help decompress any potential confrontations in your relationship, which has to be a good thing.

SENSUAL TAURUS

Your sexual connection should be expressive, sensual, and even playful, because of the youthful nature of Mercury and Virgo. If, in the past, you have been averse to trying different things in the bedroom, then Virgo, although usually virginal with most other star signs, will be prepared to explore your sensual and sexual needs, Taurus, and vice versa. This can be a very satisfactory sexual relationship, and one that is fulfilling on many other levels as well.

WORST PAIRING: TAURUS AND SAGITTARIUS

What can I say about the sexual combination between Taurus and Sagittarius, other than to warn you at the outset that your personalities are just so different? You might even find yourself asking, 'Why should I bother at all?' I guess I've jumped in boots and all, hitting you over the head with a sledgehammer before adequately explaining my reasoning for why a sexual match between Taurus and Sagittarius is just so bad! Well, here we go…

There are times when you find it difficult to express your feelings, Taurus. Many people might be forgiven for assuming this is the case, because you don't usually show how you feel until you're comfortable with a person and have gotten to know them fairly well. But this doesn't mean you don't have any feelings at all! While *we* know this to be true, Sagittarius could be one of those star signs that points the finger of emotional bankruptcy at you, condemning you for never expressing yourself. How wrong they are!

They do this based on their self-experience, and the fact that Jupiter, which rules Sagittarians, is open, jovial and, at times, quite bombastic and insensitive. Taurus and Sagittarius really are worlds apart in terms of style, life direction and long-term goals. And these distinct differences will most certainly play out in the bedroom as well.

EXCESSIVE TAURUS AND SAGITTARIUS

Taurus can be accused of being excessive due to their love of sensual things, including sex. Sagittarians also have a reputation for going over the top, but we need to draw a distinction here. Initially, you might enjoy each other's company and those all-night romps and pillow fights, but there is a different motivation between you and Sagittarius.

Sagittarius is a carefree individual who enjoys the excesses of life and lust for the purpose of sheer experience. That won't work for you, Taurus. Yes, you enjoy excess, but your fixed zodiac sign means your loyal nature needs a commitment from the other person, which your Sagittarian partner may not be able to give you. Not for a while, anyway. This will frustrate you, and the more that Sagittarius prods you to tell them what is wrong, the more you'll shut down. And so the vicious circle goes around and around.

Sagittarians will enjoy your sensual and loving attention, but they also need enough space to explore other opportunities in life, which you will not be comfortable giving them. If that's the case, you need to tell them at the outset that an open relationship is out of the question.

QUIZ: HAVE YOU FOUND YOUR PERFECT MATCH?

Do you dare take the following quiz to see just how good a lover you are? Remember, although the truth sometimes hurts, it's the only way to develop your relationship skills.

We are all searching for our soulmate: that idyllic romantic partner who will fulfil our wildest dreams of love and emotional security. Unfortunately, finding true love isn't easy. Sometimes, even when you are in a relationship, you can't help but wonder whether or not your partner is right for you. How can you possibly know?

It's essential to question your relationships and to work on ways that will improve your communication and overall happiness with your partner. It's also a good idea, when meeting someone new, to study their intentions and read between the lines. In the first instance, when your hormones are taking over, it's easy to get carried away and forget some of the basic principles of what makes for a great relationship that is going to endure.

You're probably wondering where to start. Are you in a relationship currently? Are you looking for love, but finding it difficult to choose between two or more people? Are you simply not able to meet someone? Well, there are some basic questions you can ask yourself to discover the truth of just how well suited you and your partner are for each other. If you don't have a partner at the moment, you might like to reflect on your previous relationships to improve your chances next time round.

The following quiz is a serious attempt to take an honest look at yourself and see whether or not your relationships are on track. Don't rush through the questionnaire, but think carefully about your practical day-to-day life and whether or not the relationship you are in genuinely fulfils your needs and the other person's needs. There's no point being in a relationship if you're gaining no satisfaction out of it.

Now, if you aren't completely satisfied with the results you get, don't give up! It's an opportunity for you to work at the relationship and to improve things. But you mustn't let your ego get in the road, because that's not going to get you anywhere.

The Taurus Bull is grounded and devoted. They can be a wonderful lover for the right person. As a Taurus, you need, first and foremost, a loyal person and a constant companion. So here's a checklist for you, Taurus, to see if he or she's the right one for you.

Scoring System:

Yes = 1 point

No = 0 points

- ❓ Did he/she take things slowly while dating you?
- ❓ Does he/she never rush you?
- ❓ Do you feel secure with them?
- ❓ Does he/she have a permanent and well-paying job?
- ❓ Is he/she faithful to you—do they never cheat on you?
- ❓ Is your partner a gentle mate and a peacemaker?
- ❓ Does your partner make time to be alone with you and be there when needed by you?
- ❓ Does he/she pamper you with fine, thoughtful gifts?
- ❓ Does he/she value your traditions?
- ❓ Does he/she appreciate that you mostly like to stay in one place?
- ❓ Does he/she reinforce a feeling of comfort and familiarity?
- ❓ Does he/she encourage you to analyse deeply other people's feelings and views?

- ❓ Does he/she try to encourage the expression of your emotions and spirituality?
- ❓ Does he/she ask your opinion when you both have to decide on things?
- ❓ Is he/she honest?
- ❓ Does he or she fall under the sign of Scorpio, Virgo, Capricorn or Aries?

Have you jotted down your answers honestly? If you're finding it hard to come up with the correct answers, let your intuition help and try not to force them. Of course, there's no point pretending and turning a blind eye to treatment that is less than acceptable, otherwise you're not going to have a realistic appraisal of your prospects with your current love interest. Here are the possible points you can score.

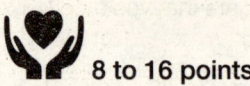

8 to 16 points

A good match. This shows you've obviously done something right, and that the partner you have understands you and is able to reciprocate in just the way you need. But this doesn't mean you should become lazy and not continue working on your relationship. There's always room to improve and make your already excellent relationship even better.

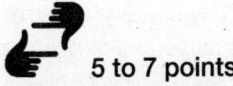
5 to 7 points

Half-hearted prospect. You're going to need to work hard at your relationship, and this will require a close self-examination of just who may be at fault. You know, it takes two to tango, and it's more than likely a combination of both your attitudes is what is dragging down your relationship. Systematically go over each of the above questions and try to make a list of where you can improve. I guarantee that your relationship will improve if given some time and sincerity on your part. If, after a genuine effort of working at it, you find things still haven't improved, it may be time for you to rethink your future with this person.

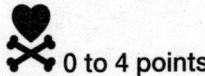
0 to 4 points

On the rocks. I'm sorry to say that this relationship is not founded on a sufficiently strong enough base of mutual respect and understanding. It's likely that the two of you argue a lot, don't see eye to eye or, frankly, have completely different ideas of what sort of lifestyle and emotional needs you each have. The big question here is why are you still with this person?

Again this requires some honest self-examination to see if there is some inherent insecurity which is causing you to hold on to something that has outgrown its use in your life. Old habits die hard, as they say, and you may also fear letting go of a relationship you have become accustomed to, even though it doesn't fulfil your needs. Self-honesty is the key here. At certain times in life you may need to make some rather big sacrifices to move on to a new phase, which will then hopefully attract the right sort of partner to you.

2012
YEARLY OVERVIEW

TIME WILL EXPLAIN IT ALL. HE IS A TALKER, AND NEEDS NO QUESTIONING BEFORE HE SPEAKS.

Euripides

KEY EXPERIENCES

The most important astrological transits throughout 2012 are those of Saturn, Uranus, Jupiter and Pluto. These planets highlight a need to carefully reassess your friendships, marital status, philosophical ideals and also your spiritual understanding of life.

Jupiter is extraordinarily lucky for you this year, Taurus, because it passes through your Sun sign. For the first time in twelve years you can expect a very significant upliftment in your personal life and relationships.

Serious responsibilities will cause you to rethink your attitudes to such things as marriage, long-term commitment and how much you are prepared to give of yourself in any deep and special relationship. The ground is shifting beneath your feet.

Career opportunities hinge on the extent to which you're able to allow your imagination to soar. Keep your feet firmly planted on the ground, but dare to dream. This will be a period when you can make your wishes a reality and achieve ambitions you previously thought impossible.

ROMANCE AND FRIENDSHIP

I'll be honest with you, Taurus: 2012 will be a challenging year for you in terms of your relationships. The intensity of Saturn will be felt most notably after September, when it enters your zone of marriage and significant personal relationships. Your responsibilities towards them might annoy you at this time.

However, you can expect some relief to arrive from the planet Jupiter, which is transiting your Sun sign throughout the whole of 2012. What this does, in effect, is soften the influence of Saturn, which would otherwise make your commitments and responsibilities in marriage quite unbearable. You need to use the influence of Jupiter to help you work through your differences in a conciliatory manner. Goodwill, humour and a sense of fairness should prevail in any of your discussions.

Uranus has an influence on your sexual appetites during the coming year or two, and this shows you'll be exploring new avenues to satisfy yourself and your partner. Actually, Jupiter is the main planet indicating your sexual activity, and it is in your Sun sign throughout most of 2012. This intimate link between sexuality and your Sun sign will be very telling on your attitudes, and shifts in your opinions, about such private matters.

The other transpersonal planet, Neptune, has much to say about your attitude to others in the coming twelve months, too. Most importantly, it rules the sign of Pisces, and for the first time in your life, it happens to be moving through its ruling zone of friendships. Many of your dreams surrounding friends, and the dreams your share with them, will come to pass. There is a karmic significance to this planet, so you'll have some unusual insights to friends specifically, but more generally about friendship satisfying a cultural need in your life.

TALK ABOUT LOVE IN 2012

You should talk about your doubts—or your interests—with a close friend. They may be able to clarify some of the things you don't normally talk about. You mustn't be scared to explore these avenues of self-expression because you'll be all that much richer for the experience.

 Relationships on the Rise

With Neptune signifying your friendships, it shows you strongly leaning towards idealism in that area of your life. You need to assess people on a practical basis rather than rushing to see something that is not there. Neptune makes an important transit after March up until May, and you will develop a new friendship with great mutual understanding at that time.

In January, Venus impacts your working life and career meaning there will be a strong tie-in with your relationships and friendships in professional activities. Those of you who are single may be surprised to meet someone in the course of your working schedule. This will be idealistic, particularly after the middle of the month.

In February, you will spend a lot of time socialising with friends. Something unusual, with someone who doesn't fit the defined character you have in mind for a partnership or friendship, will knock you off your feet. Travel is also very much on your agenda. During this period you will also need to set aside time to help an old friend with some health problems.

During March you will feel a rush of energy in the form of self-confidence, beauty and grace. You will be very attractive to potential partners, and will want to adorn yourself with lovely clothes and a new look, making you appear much more creative than usual.

August and September is a key period to reconnect and smooth over any difficulties with family and loved ones. Your artistic flair will extend to doing something different with your home and living spaces.

In November, when Saturn moves to your zone of marriage along with the Sun, you will experience some dilemma in a relationship, or will feel weighed down by commitment. Bottling things up is always a bad idea, so talk about your feelings to clear the air.

December is once again a key time, when Venus will come to the rescue, and its conjunction with Saturn will make things much better for you. Even though love will be cool, you'll get your relationship back on track. As well as this, you can look forward to gaining some valuable wisdom as a consequence.

WORK AND MONEY

Harness Your Moneymaking Powers

Making money can be summed up in an equation:

$$m (\$ \text{ money}) = e \text{ (energy)} \times t \text{ (time)} \times l \text{ (love)}$$

If one of the above factors is not present—for example, energy or love—you could still make money, but you won't be ideally fulfilled in the process.

It's absolutely essential to understand the universal laws of attraction and success when speaking about money. It is also necessary to understand that when you love what you do, you infuse your work with the qualities of attention, love and perfection.

With these qualities, you endow your work with a sort of electromagnetic appeal: a power that draws people to your work and causes them to appreciate what you do. This, in turn, generates a desire for people to use your services, buy your products and respect you for the great work you perform. This will without a doubt elevate you to higher and higher positions because you will be regarded as someone who exercises great diligence and skill in your actions.

Uranus does not sit in one of the best positions of your horoscope throughout 2012. This area relates to expenses, and with this planet expressing itself in the most unpredictable and dramatic ways, you must be very careful not to let your impulses get the better of you, particularly in the first couple of months of the year.

In February and March, Venus, your ruling planet, tends to make you justify spending lavishly. You will not necessarily just spend on yourself, either. Your generosity will prompt you to give things away and buy expensive gifts that are probably unnecessary, and you will need to analyse your motivation for doing this. You could be trying to ingratiate yourself to others due to factors of a personal nature. These would be best dealt with on a one-to-one basis, rather than throwing money at the problem.

JUPITER AND NEPTUNE IN EXCELLENT SHAPE

Jupiter and Neptune are the planets that relate to your business profits. They are both in excellent shape throughout the whole of 2012, so there's no doubt you'll be earning well. But, as the above paragraphs note, you must hold on to your money, because the secret of financial stability is not how much you earn, but how much you actually save.

Mercury, the fast-moving and intellectual planet of the zodiac, deals with your income, showing its best form in February, April and June. June will be a positive growth period for your income, and there are windows of opportunity to increase your pay or look for another job from which you can receive much greater remuneration.

Speculation pays off during September, but be careful in October and November, when debts and arguments over money are likely to arise. Have an exit strategy ready if you want to sever a business partnership, and get all the facts and figures together before entering discussions with a loved one over your—or their—poor spending habits.

To tap into your natural moneymaking abilities, use the energies of Jupiter. This means taking calculated risks, but remember that the key word here is calculated. I'm not too worried about emphasising this point to you, Taurus, because you are one of the least waste-prone star signs. Nevertheless, it's important to highlight this fact this year, because I do see you wanting to expand, and you may want to do so in a way in which you are not well enough prepared.

Think big, dare to be more speculative, and if an opportunity presents itself, don't dismiss it until you have investigated its merits a little more deeply. You'll be surprised at just how lucky you can be in these coming twelve months. The old saying, 'nothing ventured, nothing gained', is the most applicable statement to your financial forecast for 2012.

Tips for Financial Success

A few more financial and moneymaking tips can't hurt, Taurus, so here we go.

Although you must be progressive in the way you earn money, one of the karmic planets is in your zone of income until September, indicating that there may be someone you are working with who is pushing you to try new things and discard everything you have used in the past to earn money and do a good job.

Heeding their advice would be a mistake. You must not throw out the baby with the bathwater, as they say. Hang on to those procedures that have served you well and upgrade those that are redundant. This will give you the best of both worlds, and ensure excellent opportunities to extend yourself and earn more.

Until the latter part of October, Saturn's lesson for you is to consolidate your debt. By doing so, you'll be in a much better position to enjoy the fruits of your labour. This is an important tip to spare you much mental worry in the second half of 2012.

ECLIPSE HIGHLIGHT

The eclipse of the 14th of November occurs in your zone of partnerships. There will be some important matters associated with your business affiliations as a result. You will feel the pressure of someone on you and will make a change to move forward. An unacceptable partnership could hasten events.

Finally, the matter of diet, and the way it affects your energy levels for earning money. If you are running on low energy and your mind is foggy, you will not make clear, rational decisions. Rethink some of your dietary habits, because the changes you make will impact remarkably on your earning capacity.

Career Moves and Promotions

Act quickly to secure a new position in 2012. The latter half of January is an excellent time to use the position of the Sun to take hold of a new job offer or acquire another position within the company that you currently work. Your leadership abilities are pronounced in the early part of the year.

If you are unable to make a transition to a new job through a promotion or transfer, it may be more difficult for you in the second half of the year. Work hard, and use the powers of Saturn to gain a deeper insight into your industry, so that you give yourself the best possible shot at the top job.

On the 21st and the 22nd of April, when the Sun moves to your Sun sign, you'll be extraordinarily confident—this is also a time to make your move for a new position. It's a period when a fresh contract can be drawn up, or, if your current workplace agreement is not up to par, you can strike while the iron is hot, and make the appropriate changes to improve your state of mind at work.

NEGOTIATION TIME

Contracts are positive on the 21st and the 22nd of April, when the Sun transits your zone of contracts. A perfect situation to speak to your employer about improving your workplace conditions and your financial worth will then arise.

July gives you the courage to take bold new steps, possibly to travel away from your current environment and attempt something new. October and November once again bring forth the drive and ambition that give you the best possible chance against competitors or rivals vying for the same position as you.

When to Avoid Office Politics

Office politics seem to be part and parcel of work these days, so it's good to know when antagonistic, stressful days could be likely to ruffle your feathers.

On the 6th of February, be careful about how you convey your wishes and opinions on different financial matters. Others may oppose your perspective.

Gossip disturbs you throughout March. Mercury is retrograde on the 12th, so be careful not to pass on information that you have not verified first. You'll hear rumours that are upsetting. After the 24th, when Mercury moves to your social area, matters will improve.

There are challenges for you in May, after the 11th, when your relationship with a co-worker or employer reveals some flaw in your personality. Try not to get reeled in by other people's games. Head trips are the last thing you need.

Around the 21st of June you'll be slow off the mark, and could be the target of someone's bad jokes. Retain your sense of humour and you'll get through this rather difficult cycle as well.

Mars transits your zone of workplace activities after the 3rd of July. This is a contentious period, and you will be at loggerheads with those with whom you work. Keep to yourself, and don't share personal information.

Helping others is not always in your best interests, and you will learn this after the 3rd of September. Venus and Saturn create problems, and your assistance to someone could be used against you.

In October, power plays will undermine your workplace. You will need to exercise greater self-control throughout November and December, and not show your hand. Secrecy will be key to your success, even if you wish to share some of your strategies with those you still feel are friends.

HEALTH, BEAUTY AND LIFESTYLE

 Venus Calendar for Beauty

Venus brings you excellent opportunities to show off your better qualities—including your attractiveness—in January. Mostly throughout this month you will display your character through fashion statements in your professional arena.

After the 14th, there will be a shift from work to social activities, and here again your attractiveness will be noted by your peer group. New friendships will arise due to the beautiful energy of your ruling planet Venus.

With Jupiter making an important transit in the zone of your horoscope relating to your physical being, it's a no-brainer that you will be lucky in any case. However, using a little forethought about how you look, and how best to present yourself, will take your social opportunities to a new high.

MOVE OVER, SATURN!

You mustn't worry that Saturn is a considerable challenge to the way others view you, because Jupiter will no doubt soften the impact of this severe planet, and with a little bit of work on your personal grooming, makeup and fashion, 2012 should be a knockout year!

There are some setbacks in your self-esteem up until the end of June. Fortunately, the period of July to August is an excellent time to express yourself by learning the art of body language. The colour scheme you use, along with nuances of character and non-verbal communication, will be accessories to your attractiveness and ability to meet and connect with others.

Wonderful opportunities in your romantic life are indicated by the entrance of Venus into your zone of marriage in November, around the 14th. This is an important phase of your life, one in which looking your best will most certainly impact upon the quality of your relationships.

Showing off Your Taurus Traits

Each zodiac sign has its own unique power based on the elements and planets that rule it. Unfortunately, most people don't know how to tap into this power and bring out their greatest potential to achieve success in life.

You can't simply rest on your laurels in the coming twelve months, so learn to use those positive personality traits of yours to their maximum potential.

As I mentioned earlier, Jupiter transiting your Sun sign this year is a wonderful omen, giving you the opportunity to expand yourself, raise the bar, and do your best in terms of achieving success through your charm, grace and natural attractiveness.

~~LADY~~ LAZY LUCK

Although you may be lucky in January while the Sun is in your zone of good past karma, you mustn't rely wholly and solely on this aspect of good fortune. February will bring opportunities in your work and your social sphere, but by March, you will find yourself feeling down and lacking in confidence. This is where effort will be necessary to step outside your comfort zone and discover something new about yourself.

The outer expression of your personality is only the tip of the iceberg, Taurus. During the period of March to April you will discover something new about yourself, a hidden power that can be expressed very strongly in April and May. Your speech will be much more persuasive throughout these months, as I've mentioned, and this will assist you in achieving something important at this point in the year.

The months of August and September should be much more fulfilling than the previous ones. You will experience a forward movement in your life at this time and, in October, your connections with family will be more notable.

Expressing yourself becomes more important in the final two months of the year, November and December. If you bottle up your feelings there will be misunderstandings into the new year. Say what you mean and mean what you say.

Best Ways to Celebrate

When you celebrate your birthday, anniversary or another important event, it's good for friends and loved ones to understand that the Taurus temperament is not always excited about surprises, especially when too many people are possibly going to embarrass them.

Generally, you like a low-key situation with just a few close friends and family members to celebrate intimately with you. In this manner you can focus on each and every one of them without feeling as though you have overlooked anyone or not given them the attention they deserve. You hate ignoring others, especially when you know that they have, in their own loyal way, taken the time to be with you and buy you a gift.

If you would like to celebrate, a great idea is a weekend away with a close friend—possibly on a wine estate or in the natural environment—in which there is some great live music to enjoy.

February and March hold some opportunities to lift your energy, due to the transits of Venus and the Sun. Also, you'll feel surge in your mood during May, when the Sun and Jupiter connect and do their heavenly dance together.

MUSIC IN THE AIR

In August, you will have an interest in classical music, art exhibitions and live theatre. This is an opportunity for you to celebrate important occasions in a way that is, once again, a little different to the way you have done so the past.

Festive occasions for family members who are not necessarily related to you (but may have become so lately) can be enjoyed during the months from September to December. A younger person's success will be cause for jubilation in the early part of October.

KARMA, SPIRITUALITY AND EMOTIONAL BALANCE

Your most important spiritual and karmic planets are Mercury and Saturn which indicate where you can find peace and harmony in 2012.

Saturn emphasises your workplace practices up until the latter part of October. If, like most people, you get caught up in working simply for money, your peace of mind will be affected and you just won't be happy. Finding meaningful work that gives you a sense of creative expression will be part of your karmic path in the first half of 2012.

Mercury transits your zone of personal transformation and spirituality in January. You'll be working through many past issues for a new beginning in the coming twelve months. During April, when Mercury goes direct, you will understand a whole lot more about yourself. But this will only take place in a cloistered environment, by detaching yourself from your social life and the world in general.

The favourable connection between Mercury and Pluto in mid-May causes your intellect to become very penetrating, thereby allowing you to develop skills in interpersonal relationships and self-awareness.

PSYCHIC INSIGHTS

Intuitive powers are usually inborn, but there are certain transits that highlight and enhance these them. These are shown through the contacts of Mercury and Uranus after the 18th of August. You will have lightning-fast responses, and will be able to tap into a deep, universal consciousness.

Relationships help develop your spiritual wisdom. On the 6th of October, Saturn, your most important karmic planet, moves into your zone of meaningful relationships. You will be tested as to your capacity to take relationships to another level, and this will be completely dependent upon the phase of your spiritual evolution. You'll be taken to your limit. Whether you can handle this is up to you.

Once again, Mercury enters the subconscious area of your horoscope on the 21st of October, and this could be a time when you work through and resolve issues from the past. Matters of sexuality can also be part of your spiritual understanding during this phase.

You must not allow emotion to creep into your spiritual assessment of things after the 14th of November. Mercury and Neptune make you somewhat idealistic, but spirituality is always a practical affair, rather than a dream or a fantasy. If your beliefs, or the information offered to you at this time, are not practical, then discard them.

2012
MONTHLY & DAILY PREDICTIONS

EVERYONE HAS TALENT. WHAT IS RARE IS THE COURAGE TO FOLLOW THE TALENT TO THE DARK PLACE WHERE IT LEADS.

Erica Jong

JANUARY

> *Monthly Highlight*
>
> The transits of the beneficial planets Venus and Jupiter ensure a good start to the year. Excellent opportunities are likely in your professional sphere, with your vision for a new path being practically possible. Relationships are also positive for you, with your marriage planet, Mars, in the zone of romantic affairs.

1 It's best to stay indoors, with the planets indicating a very low-key period for the next day or two. This is an opportunity for you to contemplate where you want to be, and do some soul searching.

2 You're feeling lucky, but stay away from others. You'll spend plenty of time on the telephone if you don't actually socialise with friends or family members. Keeping others at arm's length is a distinct advantage today.

3 You are confident today, but there could be emotional entanglements with family members, or confusing issues that you can't really avoid. Don't let others blackmail you into doing their bidding.

4 You want to see the big picture, so you might connect with a male friend who can give you a better overview of your life. This is a perfect time to re-evaluate your philosophies.

5 Financial matters are on your mind but don't let emotion get in the way of logical and practical solutions. You may want to buy something against your better judgement.

6 Expect minor upsets, an unavoidable change or 'something different' in your family that only one of you is interested in. Go with the flow.

7 Laughter is always good medicine whenever there is a subtle tension-producing mood in the air. Have a good giggle, especially with your workmates.

8 Important documents occupy your attention today. You need to get the advice of someone who has more technical knowledge than you. Don't venture into waters that are too deep, unless you have someone on hand who can help you.

9 Beware of indulging in useless activities that will chew up a great deal of your time today. Don't allow a minor provocation to throw you off balance.

10 Being at ease and flowing harmoniously with family members brings a wonderful feeling into the dynamic of your home life. Spend a little extra time with your loved ones.

11 Real estate matters or something associated with your vehicle may trouble you today, with (in the case of the latter) confusion surrounding either its functioning or the cost of the service.

12 Even if you do not usually express much love or sentiment to your children verbally, this is a wonderful time to do so. You may feel your own inner child calling today.

13 This could be a good time to get out and meet someone new. Love is in the air, and the opportunities are boundless today.

14   Friends take on a special meaning just now, as Venus bolsters your social expressions. Don't turn down an invitation, even if you feel a little lethargic and that you might not be bothered.

15   There could be feelings of tension or awkwardness in your partnership, especially if one of you wants to know where the relationship is headed, and the other can't quite understand where the other is coming from. Clear articulation is necessary.

16   Lively conversation—and even debates—can create a rather heavy atmosphere that might creep into a work relationship today. There will be a feeling of competitiveness that could quickly shift from light humour to a more serious tone.

17   Even in the most solid of relationships there are times when you are out of sync with your loved one and thinking differently to them. Try to focus on your similarities.

18   Your partner could be quite a bit cool and aloof just now, so you will tend to be out of step with each other. Your partner's work may be weighing heavily on their shoulders.

19 Discussion of sexuality, shared resources or other investments could cause a few heated moments today. Have your facts on hand rather than shooting from the hip.

20 Taking an interest in deeper spiritual matters is likely. Someone may make comments that cause you to think differently. Sexual encounters may occur, especially if you are single.

21 Think about doing something active with your partner, but avoid spectator sports if possible. You still need some time alone to figure things out, especially if you haven't got a solid plan.

22 Your religious or philosophical interests could be reignited when you are invited to a gathering or event regarding these things. Traditional or conventional religions may be something you want to investigate.

23 The new Moon in your zone of career is significant today. A new direction can take place in your professional activities. Investigate what is on offer, and move forward with confidence.

24 You may be asked to take on a task that is quite formidable but well within your capacity. New doors are opening.

25 Friendships may be confusing at present, due to the influence of Neptune. Try not to mix business with pleasure. Draw a line in the sand to avoid misunderstandings.

26 A new friendship can commence just now, and this may arise as a result of professional connections or introductions. Don't mix business with pleasure, as they say, but by all means develop your friendships, and use your networking to improve your profitability.

27 A rumour or some malicious gossip is a problem for you. Understand the truth before you take it on board, especially if it is something surrounding a friend you usually trust. Take what you hear with a grain of salt.

28 A sudden turn of events excites you and provides the sense that life needn't be boring after all. A telephone call causes you to shift gear, and go in a new direction. Move with the flow.

29 You're worried about your weight or some other health issue, so curb your appetite for especially rich and fatty foods. Don't mix food types.

30 If you are misinterpreting a friend's messages right now—literally and figuratively—beware of blaming each other for errors that may, in fact, be imagined.

31 Don't overreact to a statement by your spouse or partner today. They may be just as emotional as you are, and it's up to you to remain cool and listen a little more than you speak.

FEBRUARY

Monthly Highlight

You can achieve an accolade for your work this month. You are bright, in control and respected by your peers and clients. Ask a friend to be clearer about their intentions, because Neptune is causing them to be a little vague. An active social life punctuates this period and makes you feel supported by the group.

1 This is a day for romantic surprises and something adventurous in the way of love, so put on your thinking cap and see what happens.

2 There may have been a change of heart in your relationship, which one of you is not aware of. It could cause a shake-up.

3 Someone from the past, or who is a little unusual, may turn up and put some pressure on your relationship today. Remain aloof and don't react.

4 You are very idealistic about your friends just now and, with Neptune influencing your social sphere, have more than likely put on your rose-coloured glasses about them. Accept your friends, faults and all.

5 You could feel frustrated that a conversation cannot be completed due to technical problems at the moment. You may need to put the discussion on hold until the universe allows better lines of communication.

6 Visiting a family relative may be difficult today, but is nevertheless a responsibility you must meet. Grin and bear it as you go through the motions.

7 A secret dalliance, an illicit affair, something taboo…These things, usually restricted to the movie screen, may actually become a reality for you today. Take a few deep breaths before you get involved in something that is difficult to get out of.

8 You may be completely at your wits' end dealing with a child, a young member of your family or the child of a friend. You may need to play hardball with them, otherwise you're going to lose respect.

9 A friend is unpredictable today and this could rile you. Rather than bottling up your feelings and fuming over the event, why not talk to them, so there's no misunderstanding about how you feel? It's up to you to express your dissatisfaction.

10 Just now you have the opportunity to focus a great deal on your professional life, and to achieve a greater measure of success. Ask for a pay rise or a better position, and if that isn't forthcoming, it could be time to seek a new job elsewhere.

11 An exhilarating day is indicated, but it could also be mentally exhausting. Get rid of your stress and anxiety by doing something sporty: get out and walk, or go to the gym and use that punching bag to release your pent-up energy.

12 Health issues are a worry. There may be something associated with your working life that is bothering you, and this is playing out in your physical aches and pains. Have a checkup and put your mind at ease.

13 Today is not the day to express too many of your heartfelt feelings. Stick to yourself, even if someone is pushing you to be a little more open and affectionate.

14 You feel unsupported by someone today, either at home or at work. The support lines of your peer group or family will be strangled or cut off. Someone may challenge, you and this will cause a great deal of grief.

15 You need to be well informed before making important choices, especially regarding your work. There could be a great deal of tension in your life just now, so it's probably a good idea simply to relax.

16 You have to rely on instincts today, because things may be a little confusing. Things are not what they seem. Someone could be play-acting a story and you're likely to believe it.

17 You have a very sensitive nature today and should use that in helping someone who has a problem. They may not express what is on their mind, but you'll have a deep sense of what's going on with them.

18 You are drawn to other cultures and will want to connect with people who are not your usual sort of friends today. Travel may be in the air. You are excited about the prospect of learning something about other countries, religions and people.

19 You can broaden your horizons now, with a tendency towards study, higher education or spiritual expansion. Going to some sort of lecture or self-help group may be timely.

20 You can't really get your ideas across to someone today, so it's best to zip your lips—do more listening and less talking. There may be some block between you and a person with whom you usually have good communication.

21 You can be very practical today, and working with others will lift your spirits. You also have an understanding of your limits and just how far you can go.

22 You can be respected emotionally in your workplace because you have a good connection with your employer. Listening carefully to their needs will allow you to provide some assistance that highlights your talents, and will open some new doors for you.

23 Communication is important today, and if business requires you to put your thoughts on paper, you can create a formidable presentation that will impress your clients or those with whom you must meet. Check your diary so you aren't double-booked.

24 There may be an opportunity to connect with a group of people—perhaps from your past—in a reunion or family get-together. This is a wonderful time to mix with others, extend your network of friends, and enjoy life.

25 You have to assert yourself in some situations, especially if others are taking advantage of you. You might need to read someone the riot act if they are taking your friendship and goodwill for granted today.

26 An important decision today could affect many facets of your life. However, you mustn't rely only on others to show you how to do things. This is a matter of self-trust, taking the bull by the horns, and boldly moving forward on your own, if necessary.

27 Empathy and the quality of your understanding will be highlighted today as you extend a helping hand to someone you know. You have to give them time as well as love to make them feel needed and confident in themselves. This is a spiritual cycle for you.

28 You have a high degree of romantic idealism as the month draws to a close. Take the time to show your affection to that special person in your life, and take the phone off the hook so you're not disturbed! There's nothing worse than interruptions when you are trying to develop personal intimacy.

29 A financial matter may occupy your mind much more than you would prefer, but you can find a solution to the problem. The trick today is to focus on something else, and not get too preoccupied by this issue.

MARCH

 Monthly Highlight

Friendships feature strongly throughout March. You're idealistic—but must also be realistic—about some of the new people you will meet. You're impulsive in your romantic affairs due to the Moon and Mars. Don't make assessments based on first impressions. You are attractive and popular because of Venus.

1 Communication is excellent again today, and positively conveying yourself to others means you can come across in a dignified manner. Lots of energy surrounds you, so this could be a time to assert yourself on some matter.

2 You could have some sort of windfall today. It is a great time for asking for a pay rise or simply enjoying the things that you have in life.

3 Don't leave routine to chance. Prepare everything methodically and double-check your appointment times. Punctuality is the key word today.

4 It's one of those days where you just don't feel like working. You will be bored and uninspired by the tasks at hand. Your in-tray could be rather overloaded. Get through the work quickly—that's the best advice.

5 You could be misunderstood today, so you need to understand where the other person is coming from. Research your topic before entering into discussion.

6 Your creativity may not flow easily today, so you will need other devices to help you to brainstorm. Don't compare yourself to others—that will make things worse.

7 Don't feel pushed to give someone an insight into your vocational plans. Competition is fierce, and someone may be trying to undermine you.

8 Take that special time with someone you love. This is an opportunity to have a night on the town and perhaps experience something a little more romantic than you had at first expected.

9 Working in a charitable way with children or other disadvantaged people is likely today. You will be appreciated for your contributions.

10 You either have to take better care of yourself or look after someone in your family today. Advising them on diet or exercise may not work, so setting an example is the best course of action.

11 Your mind and your heart don't seem to be much in sync today. Saying what you mean—and meaning what you say—may not come easily. Don't be afraid to offend someone if it's the truth.

12 Close relationships are much more powerful today and they take on a greater importance. You need to feel cared for, and if someone's not showing you affection, you need to ask them for it.

13 Your work and home lives could be at odds with each other. Or you may be taking too much work home. You need to clarify your timetable to make more time for yourself.

14 A stroke of luck is likely today, because Venus and Jupiter provide you with some good opportunities. You may receive a gift and will be very surprised.

15 Contact a long-lost friend today. Reminiscing about your past with them will be a joyous experience. A new memory will come to light and be a shared experience for both of you.

16   You are too intense trying to get your point across today. Relax and let others lead you. Be gently persuasive.

17   You could be lazy and get stuck in a rut right now. You need to motivate yourself with energising activities, food and, of course, friends. Don't become a couch potato just yet.

18   Your ego is strong today. Pull back. You needn't push others around—this could come across as a sign of insecurity. Trust others to do their jobs equally as well as you can.

19   Friendships are very powerful at this point in time. You may befriend an older person and they might give you some clarity on a general life issue.

20   You're very attractive just now as Venus, your ruling planet, conjoins the Sun. Dare to be different, and show off a little if you have to. You'll be quite attractive to potential mates.

21   Gather your energies for the new Moon shortly. Know what you want and be prepared to put it out there. A new cycle is about to commence.

22 You mustn't avoid others simply because you are nervous or apprehensive about a situation. Even if a meeting is uncomfortable today, it would be best if you participated and gave it a shot.

23 The new Moon shows that your inner and outer lives have to be in sync to be happy. Someone may detect an inconsistency in your personality. Don't let your ego fight this—you'll become a better person if you're open-minded.

24 You are highly nervous today, and need to understand that you have no control over some of the circumstances around you. Let go of your anxiety, and just trust that things will work out without your intervention.

25 You are seeking excitement due to the conjunction of the Sun and Uranus. Progressive thinking is needed, which will attract progressive opportunities to change your life.

26 Shopping for a gift, or simply getting out and about to look at new things and experience life and people, will be of interest to you today. A friend is good company, but you may get carried away with the spending.

27 You are extremely sentimental, perhaps even a little teary. Certain memories are affecting your emotions or a nostalgic movie is arousing these sentiments. It's okay to cry.

28 Don't leave your wallet, purse or valuables behind. Pay attention to where you are, or you may lose money or be swindled out of some valuables. Attend to the details.

29 You suddenly see a pattern in your financial circumstances that you didn't notice before. This can give you a great sense of relief, because things may not seem financially as bad as you had first thought.

30 An agreement based on a handshake or verbal nod may not be enough to secure the deal. The terms may change and the so-called fine print may end up being bigger than first thought. Check your contracts and agreements thoroughly.

31 It's not what you earn but what you save that makes the difference. Waste is a key issue just now, and believe it or not, you can save a lot of money just through frugality on some of the smaller things in life.

APRIL

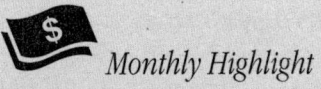 Monthly Highlight

Your finances are excellent throughout April, but don't spend more than you earn. Some sudden and unexpected expense will catch you off guard due to the Sun and Uranus. Delay a decision that involves an older sibling or a friend.

1 Don't leave domestic issues in a mess. You mustn't go to sleep angry with the one you love. Speak about the issues until a resolution's been reached.

2 Getting a valuation on your house, or looking at the financial aspects of your property, may occupy your mind just now. Research, go to auctions, and see what's happening in this sphere to get a greater understanding of it.

3 Arguments with others are likely, but that's only because you haven't been able to experience a state of non-reaction. Just because someone says something doesn't mean that you have to fall to pieces, even if it is true. Non-reaction is the key.

4 You may be accused of something that is totally untrue. How are you going to act on this? You either need to be able to prove yourself with facts, or discard the issue completely. You're never going to please everyone all of the time.

5 A creative streak is indicated as the Moon and Mercury influence your mind. Stop everything and do something that allows you to express yourself. It will be thoroughly fulfilling.

6 Work methods can take on a whole new spin as someone changes the rules on you. 'Shape up or ship out' seems to be the message of the Sun and Uranus at present.

7 You're serious about your work but you cannot hold on to outdated methods. Someone is trying to outdo you—you can either compete or continue to work at your own pace.

8 Love seems to be full of entanglements for you at the moment, but only because you are not seeing things from the other person's point of view. You need to be cold and calculating before reaching an emotional space that is more fulfilling.

9 You probably don't often think about it, but people can be jealous of you at times. If this comes to your attention, it will change your attitude towards someone you thought was more supportive.

10 You can feel the pulse of the city, or at least of the community that you live in just now. Express an interest in others, and take part in some celebration that involves a lot of people.

11 Issues of karma will be uppermost in your mind. If you've played your cards right, then some good fortune can come to you. If you've held back, then the universe will be doing the same.

12 If you are a woman reading this, understanding the behaviour your parents will go a long way to helping you to improve your own relationships just now. Look at the past with a clear mind.

13 You are in an extremely generous mood at the moment, but don't be too generous—others may misinterpret your motives. Go slowly, and people will be able to receive what you are offering in measured doses.

14 Once again, the Moon swings around into your career sector. Don't get too emotionally involved in the work you do. Create a bit of space around yourself and the quality of your work will be much better.

15 An employer could express personal intentions towards you and you can become friendlier with them, and more respected. However, don't be too quick to accept.

16 Don't get between two friends who are having a brawl right now. Mediation won't work, and will only serve to distance you from both of them.

17 You can think up creative new ways to be profitable, especially if you run an independent business or are developing a hobby into a more serious career concept. Don't be afraid to think differently.

18 This is a good time to work on an uncommon proposal. Assess the value of your ideas from an unconventional angle and you'll silence your critics.

19 You are moving too fast for your own good. Words may come out of your mouth before you have a chance to think about what you're saying. Great for creativity, but bad for business.

20 The Sun now returns to your Taurean Sun sign, indicating a boost in energy levels and self-confidence. Share your joy and sunshine around with a few good friends. This should be a good day.

21 It's time to shake off the old you and recreate yourself. The new Moon prods you to try on some new clothes, get a new hairstyle and experiment with some new makeup and colours. Your charm is strong today—use it well.

22 Be wary of misplacing affections. You may want to see the best in someone only to find out later that all that glitters is not gold.

23   There are quick words—and even angry thoughts—coming to light. You have considerable speed in your typing and a **dexterous** approach to your work. You might be impressive to your employer today.

24   You may get tongue-tied at the most inappropriate moment today. If you're not sure what to say, or are in a meeting with new people, it's best to say less.

25   Don't fast-track a romantic involvement, even if you have the sense that it's meant to last. Play it safe and get to know the person a little better first.

26   A day for great communication and connection with others. If you haven't been talking much to friends, revive the discussions and the enjoyment.

27   Your interactions with women are strong. Reconnect with the feminine side of your nature, even if you happen to be a man.

28   Being cramped or constrained in your home means you need to create more space. Spend time removing the clutter so you can breathe the fresh air of your own company.

29 You can't go backwards, Taurus. If a job offer or friendship that you previously let go of once again seems appealing, say no.

30 There is value in something you've discarded. Maybe it's cheap and you're looking for a bargain? You may be able to stretch a penny quite a long way today.

MAY

Monthly Highlight

You have a stroke of luck for which you can thank the Sun and Jupiter this month. Speculation is excellent, and your investments are likely to pay off handsomely. Watch your weight, because Jupiter shows you starting to add on a few kilos. Exercise, diet and other health issues should be at the top of your agenda.

---

1 The month kicks off with some wonderful romantic and sexual energy. The Moon and Mars make you impulsive, but just be careful that you don't overstep the bounds of good faith.

2 Pick up a new sport today, because Mars endows you with considerable physical vitality. However, don't push yourself beyond your limits, otherwise you may cause yourself injury.

3 The Moon is in your sixth zone of health. Work and other daily routines may cause you to become frazzled. Plan effectively to get through your tasks.

4   You're wasteful at work, or overextending yourself in areas that you don't need to be involved. Stick to the task at hand for best results.

5   Your communication with your colleagues and others in your business community will pay off today. Write business letters and proposals now because Mercury is on your side.

6   The Sun returns to its base position, indicating an immense level of self-confidence. Go for what you want, and ask for favours that you've postponed.

7   You are humorous and have a quick wit just now. Don't get too serious about things, even if there are pressing issues at hand.

8   Don't rush your chores today, because you may cut corners and find yourself having to retrace your steps. You are also being scrutinised by someone you are unaware of.

9   You may find yourself doubting your professional path at the moment. There's no harm in changing, but not for change's sake alone. Get back to the core of what first drew you to your career.

10 You have excellent powers of conveying your creative ideas to friends and business associates, but be sure to keep it practical.

11 You're at odds with your boss or a superior in your workplace. If you want to say something to them, it may be better to send an e-mail or text message. Avoid confrontation.

12 This is the perfect day to go for a job interview or, if you wish to be well received by others, to present yourself and look forward to success. This is the start of a new cycle.

13 You are sharp verbally, but be careful that others don't accuse you of being a smarty pants. Underplay your knowledge of a certain subject.

14 You have an investigative mind and will be called upon to research a difficult topic. You will uncover some additional information that will be useful to you in another area of your life.

15 You have an insight into a character fault of a friend, but may be too scared to say anything about it. Are you interested in helping them? Well, you may just need to tell them the truth.

16 Venus moves retrograde and this has something to say about your relationships just now. There may be some mistrust surrounding a partner or friend.

17 You could be drawn to doing something that pushes your physical body to its limits. The better approach would be to watch a high-impact, fast-paced movie to avoid injuring yourself.

18 Studious activities are appealing. Read a book or expand your knowledge to improve your skills—not just professionally but in your personal life as well.

19 You may accidentally misrepresent yourself, or be misrepresented by someone on your staff. Be clear about what you want before people go out to do your bidding. You can avert an embarrassment.

20 The next month will be primarily focused on money, earnings and how you can maximise the use of your money. Get some assistance or advice on how to best invest your money.

21 The solar eclipse occurs in your zone of material values. You'll need to rethink what's important to you, and this may go against the values of some of your family members. You must be true to yourself, remember that.

22 Something you say, albeit casually, may have a profound impact on someone whose company you happen to be sharing. You'll be surprised at how much you influence their thinking and life.

23 You may undergo a mini identity crisis just now. But this can be averted through your connections with a new group of people. Be true to yourself.

24 You may disapprove of a friend's spiritual or philosophical opinions. Politics may also be under scrutiny, so don't let this develop into an argument or, worse still, a parting of the ways.

25 You have a clever moneymaking scheme in the back of your mind. Discuss this with a friend you trust, but if strangers are in your company, it's best to postpone discussions until later.

26 You'll be forgetful today, and not just with valuables but with the most mundane things: your handkerchief, cosmetics or other bits and pieces you normally take for granted.

27 You have the opportunity to make money from a secondary source, but if you think carefully about this, you may not have time to do it. If you accept the proposal, you may find yourself overwhelmed. Don't do too much.

28 There is a greater feeling of ease in work matters as Venus creates a favourable aspect to your workplace. You may meet someone influential in assisting you to go the next step professionally.

29 It's a technological sort of day, and one in which you can pat yourself on the back. You may learn something in the way of computing, such as a new application, which will help you immensely.

30 In a strange sort of way, you might make a friend who is very different in character to your usual peers. At first you'll be apprehensive, but you will soon learn to like this person, and may even start to adopt some of his or her mannerisms.

31 It's an argumentative type of day, with Mercury and Mars giving you no comfort. Bite your tongue, even if you feel you've got something useful to say.

JUNE

Monthly Highlight

You are likely to be inundated with work, and could be distracted due to your desire to earn money and reduce your debts. But don't let this run you ragged. Balance your work life with sufficient down time to give you rest and peace of mind. Mars continues to make you sexually exciting.

---

1 You feel artistic today, and you can thank Mercury and Venus for that. Try your hand at writing some poetry, playing an instrument or painting. You'll discover a new part of yourself.

---

2 If you've been waiting on a communication relating to work or another kind of service, the letter or e-mail could arrive today. This is an excellent cycle for communication.

---

3 Slow and steady wins the race, as shown by Mercury and Saturn. Take your time with your work and don't be hurried by others. You can expect a good outcome and some deep satisfaction from the work you do.

4 You are feeling energetic once again, so it's time to do those physical tasks and jobs around the house you've been postponing for a while. Brace yourself and tuck your tummy in, especially if you're bending and lifting things.

5 A lunar eclipse occurs in your zone of sexuality, revealing many new things about your partner, even if you've known them for a long time. Dare to try something different.

6 Neptune is retrograde today and influences your friendships and your social aspirations. You may need to postpone that dream you've had for yourself and a friend.

7 Mercury enters your zone of travels, so many short journeys are likely both today and in the next few days. You needn't rush—just take your time and enjoy the trek.

8 Injuries are likely if you rush things. Arguments are likely if you push your opinions on to others. Frustration is likely if you don't accept yourself. Be gentle and all things will work out in your favour.

9. You must bridge the gap between the vision you have for your life and the practical application of those ideas. You may be living in two worlds today, and the secret is to plug the practical into the mystical.

10. The Sun offers you greater opportunities and flexibility in your workplace. If you need to take work home, ask yourself if this is going to make life easier on the home front.

11. You may need to support someone who is not exactly a great friend. If there's competitiveness in the workplace, you may just have to accept that this is an unwritten rule of business and etiquette. Your turn will come.

12. Jupiter's entry into your zone of income occurs for the first time in twelve years. You're up for some extraordinarily opportunistic financial scenarios. Dare to think big and big things will happen.

13. You could be on edge today and every little thing will trigger your reactions. Youngsters—particularly if you have children—will grate on your nerves, maybe even make you explosive. On the upside, some intuitive flashes prompt you to act.

14 You can't quite get your thinking straight today. Even though you're able to work well, you can't connect the dots. There's no shame in asking someone to give you a hand, especially if they know better.

15 Apply for that new course, and if your employer is willing to subsidise you, then you should definitely consider expanding your mental horizons. This is a great educational cycle.

16 You may be causing your own health problems at the moment, by worrying about things you can't change or over which you have no control. Lighten up a little, and deal with each problem one at a time.

17 You may be worried about spending more than you had allocated on a gift or an item of clothing. Gift yourself, and understand that the very act of being generous to yourself gives the universe permission to provide you more in return.

18 Avoid sugar today. It may make you hyperactive and affect your emotional responses regarding both relationships and financial decisions. Find a healthy substitute.

19 You'll feel really connected to a friend today and can revel in the joys of your association. There may be some aspects of their relationship that you can help them with.

20 It's a new Moon, and once again we see strong connections between planetary forces and your finances during this part of the year. Continue to develop your ideas, and have no fear of making changes now that should, after all, carry you to the next phases of your financial and professional lives.

21 There's a greater connection—or perhaps reconnection—with siblings at the moment. Find common ground to enjoy common roots. You can bury the hatchet if you've previously had problems with them.

22 Your co-operation is accentuated, and you can support your partner in achieving a new level of awareness. Your encouraging words will go a long way in helping them to regain confidence.

23 A bizarre twist of fate could put you in touch with a person who is exciting enough to cause you to do something foolish. You need to balance the tried and tested with the unknown today.

24 Events in your environment could make you angry or confused. Don't get too caught up in the larger scheme of things, and remember that although you are a small piece of the universal puzzle, what you do can make a difference. It's all in your attitude.

25 Practical affairs that have been on hold move forward just now, much to your amazement. You thought you'd never turn the corner, but it's happened! Don't be too pushy, though. Things could still take a little bit of time.

26 Changes are afoot in your domestic sphere. For some Taureans, this could herald an interest in moving house or travelling. However, don't be impulsive.

27 It's time for some fun back home. Invite friends over, cook a sumptuous meal and enjoy some fine wine in the midst of friends. This should be a relaxing day.

28 Venus goes direct this month, and today relationship struggles finally seem to come to an end, or, at least, you reach some new conclusion. Enjoy the company of your partner without digging up the past.

29 Buy a car or the lavish, luxurious item that's been on your mind for a while. It may cost a little more than you had anticipated but will be worth it, and you can always pay the credit card off next month.

30 The Sun, Mercury, Jupiter and Uranus combine to bring you a smorgasbord of events akin to a rollercoaster ride. Keep things on an even keel, and don't exaggerate matters today.

JULY

Monthly Highlight

Work matters continue to bother you. You could have a falling out with a workmate or an employer—don't let things build up to an unmanageable level. Home issues can bring you satisfaction, and there is an opportunity to reconnect with relatives and other friends. A celebration at home brings a lot of joy.

1 Sexuality, and sharing your intimate secrets with a loved one, will be the focus today. However, if you don't express these feelings, you will be frustrated.

2 Your desires on some level will be unfulfilled. Try to accept where you are for the time being without expecting more than your fair share. All good things come to those who wait.

3 You are too idealistic about a situation just now and need to get real. Wishing something or someone to be a certain way is not going to make it a reality.

4 Memories of the past linger, a mixed bag of feelings as you try to decipher where you are at the moment. You could feel exploited by someone who is taking advantage of you either financially or emotionally.

5 You are like a dog at a bone today, trying to get to the bottom of an issue, and in the process: irritating someone close to you. There is always another approach available to reach a goal, so try a little subtlety.

6 You're working too hard and should realise you can overdo it. Late or sleepless nights, poor dietary habits, and too much worry over incidental issues could cause you injury or illness.

7 Meeting with in-laws or people you're uncomfortable hanging out with could be a problem today. The difficulty is that there may be no way out of the dilemma. Hang in there. All things must pass.

8 You may not be able talk about issues surrounding your work, even to someone you trust. What you are experiencing may actually be a projection of your own state of mind. Think about that.

9 Doing a favour while begrudging it is a really bad form of karma. A friend may ask you to help them and you won't feel comfortable about it.

10 You need someone to assist you today, but may feel as if you are imposing on their time. It seems to be the opposite of yesterday.

11 Charity begins at home, and if you've been too busy out and about helping this or that person, you may have overlooked the fact that someone near and dear requires more help than you think.

12 A flash of brilliance today gives you the inspiration to move forward on an idea. Irrespective of what friends or family have to say about it, you should trust your instincts and do what you feel is right. Eventually this could make money.

13 You have a million and one ideas today, but may not know where to begin. It could be one of those days where you are so busy that you actually get nothing done. Draw up your list and systematically work through it.

14 You're tougher today and will be able to better balance the male and female aspects of your personality. This is important, especially if you have to act in the role of mediator.

15 Your sense of appreciation is much greater today, and you will realise just how much you have. Having this attitude of gratitude helps in improving your relationships with the people you love.

16 You might be looked up to by your peer group today. Taking on the role of mentor will naturally bolster your self-confidence.

17 You can think big today—don't let anyone tell you that there is such a word as impossible. Be careful of spending too much, however, because you may later regret it.

18 Your communication relies a great deal on your intuition. You may not feel completely comfortable meeting someone for the first time. Your first impression will probably be correct.

19 There is too much intense, aggressive energy around you today. Mars and Pluto are in no mood to make it easy for you. Someone could even become verbally abusive.

20 The gift of the gab is a wonderful thing. But there's no use relying on it if you're not going to put it into practice in the first instance. Make the most of it.

21 A journey may reluctantly be taken, but it is an essential part of your work schedule. Plan well in advance, and make sure you haven't double-booked yourself.

22 The new Moon occurs, giving you a fresh approach to communication and learning. You may feel like taking up a new subject— not necessarily to impress others, but just as a matter of curiosity.

23 Your common sense may not be appreciated today. It confounds you when this happens because of your Taurean sensibilities. Stick to the plan.

24 This is a lucky day in which you may win money or an accolade. In any case, Jupiter and Uranus are giving you a taste of good fortune, and I say go with it while you're still on a roll. A small gamble can be fun.

25 You're quick on the uptake today, so you'll need to be with people who have a certain amount of intellectual brilliance and communicative links. You'll die if you're in boring company. Choose friends wisely.

26   If you keep looking at a cup as being half empty, you may miss the fact that there is anything in it at all. Stop focusing on the debt, and look at the assets that you have.

27   If you overplay your talents in a workplace scenario, you may be asked to bite off more than you can actually chew. Try to be a little humble.

28   There may be an unusual power of attraction to someone with whom you do business with just now. If you're able to contain this power it could develop into a fruitful friendship, but don't push it beyond this.

29   You could be nervous about finishing a job or project, or an essay if you are a student. The trick is to break it down into its constituent parts, and not get overwhelmed by the total job.

30   You could be flying high today, either figuratively or literally. Uranus provides you with zest and energy, but ideas of radical reform may be met with resistance.

31   There can be tension in your relationships today. You may suddenly want to shift direction in an existing romantic affair, but doing this will still leave you high and dry.

AUGUST

Monthly Highlight

You are very frustrated this month, so be careful not to let your emotions impact on your health. Previous antagonism from a co-worker finally needs to be resolved. Health issues could reach a crisis point. Get a medical checkup to make sure everything is okay, and learn to meditate so you can decompress from any stressful situations.

1 There is a love of freedom in your workplace today. Be careful not to step on people's toes, because a regimental environment is not your cup of tea. You will challenge authority over an issue.

2 You need to avoid problems in relationships by getting to know someone a little better. Forming any new association just now requires less impulse and more analysis.

3 You may come across an unstable personality today. Reserve judgement and, better still, don't talk about this to third parties. It may produce problems for you.

4 A pleasant journey characterises today, and possibly the next couple of days. Cultural excursions are on the cards. Travel with a friend.

5 You'll be rather angry and frustrated and may not be able to connect with others today. If you know you're going to lash out, it's best to stay indoors.

6 Don't allow friends to coerce you. By sticking to your own schedule you'll feel that much better, and they will respect you for it.

7 If you can do your work in a quiet environment, you'll get much more done. Setting up a home office is really not a bad idea.

8 You could have a breakthrough today and, after considerable challenges or obstacles from those around you, this will be a welcome relief. A practical ideal will start to take shape.

9 Mercury now moves forward in your horoscope, and it will now have a great deal to do with your finances. If you previously had to postpone a decision, now is the time to act boldly.

10 You may end up leaving a few people behind, but if you race ahead of the crowd, you could find yourself alone. Team spirit is essential.

11 Some sort of romantic ideal could start to come through for you just now, either in the form of meeting a new person who fits the description of your dreams, or in the manifestation of a desirable situation in your current relationship.

12 You could be lax in some of your financial affairs, and will need to spend extra time going over the books. Pay more attention to detail, and don't be distracted socially.

13 Mars continues to be a thorn in your side at work, particularly in its relationship to Saturn. You're damned if you do, and you're damned if you don't.

14 Connections with neighbours can go one of two ways: you need to make peace or avoid them all together. Consuming milk or dairy products doesn't seem like a good idea today.

15 Don't rush to your destination. Don't speed in the car. Zip your lips. Be calm, patient, and avoid injury.

16 Spend time with your mother or an older female in your family. There is something to be gained through discourse with this person.

17 Travel northwards if you have to—this direction gives you good fortune today. A friend from that area may have a surprise for you.

18 A new Moon is fortuitous and shows a change of pace, particularly in reference to your home life. Some new furnishings may be desirable.

19 A competitive spirit beckons you to take up a sport or do some running or vigorous exercise. Time to join the gym if you're not yet a member.

20 Pay some of your debts now or they will bother you for the next few weeks. It may be hard, especially if it means sacrificing something that you want.

21 You need to be patient with someone who is much slower than you. They could be a new person at work who just doesn't get it. Patience is a virtue.

22 Don't let frustrations build up. You need to change your attitude towards a person who is not compatible with you. Don't withhold your opinions.

23 You can feel an increase in love and passion. Is your partner feeling the same, though? That is the question. You may need to quiz them on why they seem so distant.

24 Your self-confidence could meet resistance with another dominant character today. Both of you possess qualities of leadership, but who is going to be the humble one?

25 You'll experience a great deal of energy from teamwork today. Success can be achieved by associating with groups of people, rather than going it alone.

26 Don't overestimate yourself today, Taurus. Be frank, and express your need for integrity. But don't push your truth too hard, or others may lose respect for you.

27 You have a lucky chance just now, so don't blow it. You may need to express another side of your personality to make a convincing argument.

28 If you are unmarried, this could be a period where you feel an urge for family or children. In any case, you could be associated with nursing mothers or more family-oriented activities.

29 You may need to take a break from work rather suddenly to recharge your batteries. You don't need to explain yourself to anyone: it's your business and only yours.

30 You could have the desire to enter into a new relationship or partnership, but you mustn't be impulsive. There are some elements of disharmony in this newfound love.

31 Don't let dark thoughts overtake you. A pessimistic outlook is not going to win you friends. The last thing people want to hear is your problems.

SEPTEMBER

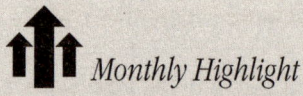 *Monthly Highlight*

A more active personal life is on the agenda, but this could also indicate that you are less likely to accept the wishes of your partner or spouse. Disputes over directions or ideals seriously need to be addressed. Youngsters are very much in your field of vision, bringing you a lot of happiness. Sport and other outdoor activities are a great relief from your usual working life.

1 Analytical thinking may throw you out of whack today, because you'll be too busy worrying about the details rather than enjoying yourself. Make time to get out and live life.

2 Choices between friends or lovers become a problem if you are not clear on their personalities. If this is a romantic issue, you will need to be shrewd to come to a conclusion.

3   You may need to be separated from someone even though you love them. Don't look at this is a bad thing because absence does indeed make the heart grow fonder. Learn to appreciate what you have.

4   Don't let emotional frustrations express themselves as anger. If you can't talk just now, send a note or an e-mail outlining your thoughts. This will document your feelings without ambiguity.

5   You mustn't get in the way of people working out their problems. Even if a battle becomes fierce, it's best to mind your own business and not get embroiled in what could be a long, drawn-out dispute.

6   Someone may try to embarrass you today, but you'll be a step ahead of them. You probably already know that someone is envious of you, trying to catch you out to make you look foolish.

7   It may be hard to find your feet today, but leaning on someone else may not be the way to go.

8   If you are negligent of your duties, you have no one else to blame for the difficulties that result. Pay special attention to your obligations and act on them now.

9 You are vital today and will need the company of someone equally as energetic. They say that if you hang around someone who is a cripple, you will develop a limp.

10 You need a little mischievousness in your life today, an opportunity to let your inner child out. But don't be too silly about things. Enjoy yourself.

11 Your imagination is at an all-time high at the moment. However, you will need to find the right mechanisms to manifest these impulses.

12 There are some aspects of your personality that are uncontrollable at the moment. Is this hormonal? Is there anything you can do about it? Think before you act.

13 You may find yourself in the company of people who have a rather peculiar disposition towards sex and morals. Listen and learn.

14 Today is a day of tidying up, putting things in order, and figuring out where your valuables may be. This will help you become more efficient.

15 Use your creative powers to overcome a problem just now. Creativity is not simply about painting, music or drama.

16 It's time to make some far-reaching plans in your life, so that you can execute a strategy to achieve your dreams. But only share these ideas with people who will support you and help you become successful.

17 You can attain something amazing today, but remember that the secret of great success is to share your successes with others. The more you give, the more you'll get.

18 Recently, you felt you needed to be particularly resistant to someone's push for change. Resistance will cause problems, but if you are diplomatic in your attitude, you can get through this.

19 You have the ability to share your happiness today and lift the spirits of someone who may be down in the dumps.

20 You'll be feeling lively and particularly communicative when in the company of friends today. You mustn't allow this situation to become too competitive.

21 You have intensified feelings of love for someone just now, but they may not be reciprocated. Unfortunately you might have to endure disappointment to get to the truth.

22 Where there is a will, there is a way. Mercury and Jupiter indicate that you can communicate ideas, put forward bold new plans, and get the support you need from others today.

23 You may not be able to make a decision easily if someone is breathing down your neck. Disappear for a while, and get your thinking clear before coming back to them.

24 You have the opportunity to meet someone who has considerable influence, perhaps even someone reasonably well known in the community. Use this opportunity to gain some leverage.

25 You can be successful if you're starting a business. Make sure you have your plans in order and that you've made all the relevant consultations to ensure this is a smooth process.

26 You need to exchange thoughts with someone who has a love of social and cultural activities. If you're stuck in a rut with your peer group, not being satisfied is going to be very frustrating.

27 You may expect a meeting to be unconstructive and so will be quite surprised when others receive your opinions gracefully. You will walk out of it with more self-confidence.

28 You'll deal with sensitive or sick people today, who will be appealing to your empathy. Nevertheless, you must remain strong if you are going to help them improve.

29 Don't act impulsively today, even though you are still in the mood to help others. You could get caught off guard with a hard-luck story—a ploy to fleece you of your money.

30 Don't let excessive ambitions rule on the work front. Explain your intentions so that people don't feel threatened.

OCTOBER

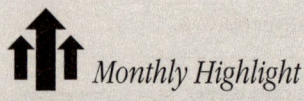

Monthly Highlight

Saturn makes its presence felt in your zone of personal and marital relationships. This is the start of a very serious and responsible cycle in your love life. Talk about your frustrations, and don't let issues build up. Jupiter's influence still gives you the opportunity to smooth things over and to get your relationships back on track. Work is positive as well.

1 Today, feel encouraged to transform your personality into something that will make an impact on others professionally and personally. Just do it.

2 You're in for an intense day where crosscurrents and confused signals won't necessarily create peace. You are out of step with others and don't like their dance.

3 People are prepared to listen to your advice today. A token of appreciation will restore your faith in a friendship. Fewer words will have a greater impact.

4 Your personality really will shine today, with your self-confidence inspiring everyone with whom you come in to contact.

5 A blast from the past unexpectedly drops in on you, but you realise just how different you've become. The mood turns cool.

6 Don't let being judgemental get in the way of open-hearted communication. It's best to leave meetings in the nostalgia basket if you don't want to develop a friendship any further.

7 It's time to speak up about what you want and stop eating humble pie. Demand your fair share of the glory in any success. You can be a leader and feel confident in a job well done.

8 Changes in your residential situation are on the cards just now, but you may not know where to begin. Try window-shopping to get a feel for style and price before committing to anything.

9 Don't react too strongly if, when trying to put forward your opinion today, it differs from others. A sensitive issue affects you because of past memories.

10 Your career could be in for a topsy-turvy ride, with changes in your workplace inevitable. You are not calling the shots and it bothers you.

11 Anything associated with your work—including your employer, the type of work you do and the people you work with—will be spotlighted today. It may not leave much time for anything else.

12 Take appropriate precautions to clarify your position if you foresee a challenge to your status on the work front. Confide in your boss.

13 You might already be considering various changes, and now will be the time when you are nudged, if not pushed, by destiny to do what your heart is suggesting.

14 Some news may not necessarily mean a permanent change, but additional responsibilities will cause alterations in your daily schedule. Taking on an additional responsibility is annoying.

15 The new Moon today has much to say about your love affairs. You feel an upswing in both your desire to be affectionate and for it to be reciprocated. A new romance commences.

16 Today, you need to delegate tasks if possible. If you have someone in mind to do the work, they may not be too happy when you provide them with the schedule.

17 You mustn't let bad vibes overtake your reasonable discussions, even if you feel like strangling someone. Understand that they may be going through a bad time, and it is not totally their fault.

18 You need to avoid alcohol and late nights during this phase, because it can radically affect your judgement and health. You need to face up to any problems fairly and squarely today.

19 Take stock of yourself, and send off any important letters and documents to finalise negotiations. If taxation issues or other financial loose ends are bothering you, clear them up now.

20 You can certainly mix business and pleasure today. The opportunities are boundless. Introductions bolster your ego and give you a taste of how the other half lives.

21 You may find yourself working with people quite junior in age, but this will be a welcome relief from your habitual routine. Enjoy the change of pace.

22 Your physical looks and charm play a large part in drawing people to you today. You have power over others now, and you know it. Just don't abuse it.

23 Artistic pursuits are strong today, and you could choose to take up an artistic pastime to channel these energies.

24 You will have a couple of hurdles today, but they will be cleared up quickly. Don't dwell on the negative but focus on the positive aspects of your relationships.

25 I foresee you meeting someone from a completely different background who will open your eyes to alternative possibilities. Dreaming of a new life is exhilarating.

26 Your travel urges are strong and now is the time to make plans (even if you don't actually board a plane or boat). Talk to a friend about your travel aspirations.

27 You can't sit still today because Uranus makes you feel as if you have ants in your pants. Get outdoors rather than staying in. You won't accomplish much behind a desk.

28 You need love this month and today you will actively seek it. Just don't ingratiate yourself and appear to be a beggar.

29 You're stirring up some reasonably big ideas today, but you needn't pursue these pathways by throwing money at a concept before testing it.

30 You may feel as if you are being selfish just now, but how are you going to help others if you don't help yourself first? Your need to be compassionate has to be balanced.

31 A test of friendship is likely, but you may not be in the mood for games at the moment. This could cause you to drift further from someone who was once a good friend.

NOVEMBER

Monthly Highlight

Figuring out a strategy for your shared money and resources is a great idea this month. Additional responsibilities on your partner's shoulders may require you to step up to the plate and lend a hand. Don't argue about money, and try to find some practical solutions that are agreeable to both of you.

1 I see that your efforts today will not be completely limited to worldly or material achievements. You have deeper and more significant issues that you wish to tackle, and may have to do this alone.

2 There can be unexpected yet pleasant changes in relationships today. You may experience some excitement when it comes to meeting a new person through an introduction.

3 By looking at the workings of your mind and reducing mental tension, you can avoid long-term problems. Relationships will benefit immensely through some self-analysis.

4   If you've been stalling on a dental or medical procedure, this month is a good time to do it. You don't necessarily have anything wrong, but it is always better to be safe, than sorry.

5   You are likely to form quite a few new social contacts, and they will lead to pleasant meetings with others who have similar interests to you.

6   Don't allow stresses within your love life lead to a separation from the one you love. It's quite likely that friendships outside the relationship are having an influence over you or your partner.

7   Watch out for deliberate acts of deception from others. It's quite likely, due to your lack of self-awareness, that you are missing vital clues as to who are friends and who are not.

8   You'll be able to relate to children very easily today, and this will reciprocate a great deal of happiness. Creativity is also heightened, and your appearance will be pleasing to your friends and lover.

9   You can actively participate in joint work projects because this will be a really constructive period. You have the vision and the energy to start and finish great work.

10   A co-operative endeavour will spill over into your social life and stressful times will disappear.

11   Your career may improve, and your chosen line of work will give you satisfaction. Don't stay in a position that no longer fulfils your creative urges.

12   If you are working or studying, this will be a period of promotion, better marks and all-round approval for your work.

13   You could feel as if you are under the control of someone else, possibly an authoritarian figure or a family member. Don't allow other people to limit your life.

14   It's time to communicate with determination and intention what you really want in life. The new Moon indicates a turning point that others may not appreciate, but one which you must instigate.

15   You will think very rapidly on your feet today, with a desire to tackle new projects. You have the capacity to start a new business or to try something completely different.

16   This is a popular, successful time in your life where there is a lot of inner fulfilment. You'll be open to sharing what you have earned with others. Generosity is the key today.

17 A state of emotional transition is likely now, so expect several critical developments in your romantic affairs. Reacting to someone else's over-reaction only creates greater tension. Keep your cool.

18 There can be blocks in communication, especially where sexuality and/or money play a role. Don't play power games relating to these issues—this will only escalate the drama in your life.

19 There will be additional responsibilities thrust your way, but you will instead be tempted to throw all cares to the wind. It may indeed give you a breath of fresh air to commence something new.

20 It's time to connect with people who will improve your station in life. This means meeting and networking with a new group of individuals. There is a strong social flavour to the transits just now.

21 There is the real possibility of meeting a soulmate during this period of the year. You have the capacity to fulfil and be fulfilled at the moment. Consider online dating services.

22 Sugar-coat your words, and don't be forceful when twisting someone's arm to bring them around to your way of thinking. You needn't achieve everything today.

23 You could meet someone with whom you've had a past-life connection. There will be an immediate rapport with this individual, and your feelings could deepen for each other.

24 An emotional experience with an employer will have a positive and uplifting effect on your workplace situation, improving your mental attitude.

25 There may be some retaliation within a relationship, which makes you very volatile today. You probably have good reason to feel like this, but find a way to calm the situation.

26 You'll still be feeling a tremendous buzz and vitality, but impatience or intolerance regarding those who aren't as quick off the mark as you could cause arguments.

27 Expect fun times at work, but that will depend on how quickly you finish the job so that there are no outstanding responsibilities. Take the initiative and be part of the group today.

28 You can expect to be hauled into a social event that requires your expertise today. Don't be too quick in coming forward because you may end up with more than you bargained for.

29 Don't take to mimicking others' speech patterns, because it will be obvious you've been hanging around with someone for far too long.

30 You'll be flighty and impatient and finding it extremely hard to sit still today. It's not at all a good idea to schedule a lengthy coffee with a friend if you're feeling this hyperactive.

DECEMBER

Monthly Highlight

Your focus is making a great impression on everyone around you in the final month of the year. Mercury, Venus and Saturn indicate that you are plugged into public relations, friends and lovers, and also want more serious discussions generally. Mars and Pluto activate your desire to travel, and this could indicate a significant journey with important spiritual ramifications.

1 You might receive false information that will lead you into an argument over a financial matter or business issue. Try to keep a level head, and have your facts handy.

2 Ignore false messages that haven't got any basis in truth, because they will only cause you to retaliate, creating further problems for yourself and others.

3 Expect setbacks in travel, business or other communications, but don't write off the situation just yet. Plan B will need to be implemented at a future date.

4 Just when you thought the coast was clear, a surge in passion could return to create difficulties in your relationships. Sidestepping is a useful thing.

5 You'll be feeling emotional, if not over-reactive, to your partner's words and actions today. Use humour to diffuse any potential arguments before they get started.

6 Someone's view doesn't have a ring of truth just now. However, try to listen to their side of the story before shooting from the hip, even if it sounds too good to be true.

7 Focus again on your sexual intimacy, because this part of your life will be highlighted at the moment. If your partner is not amenable to joining in, you'll need to increase your appeal.

8 If you've complained about being less than happy in your love life, you'll be surprised when your lover or spouse pays extra attention today.

9 Too many unexpected tasks won't sit comfortably today, because you're feeling highly strung and incapable of dealing with work and other activities. De-stressing is essential.

10 You're likely to gain the appreciation of your boss just now by being quietly assertive rather than voicing your opinions. Any suggestions you might have should be expressed through the written word.

11 Whatever you do today will be brilliant and captivate the imagination of others. You mustn't be afraid, even if it seems a little impossible. You can only try.

12 You may have some personal obligations you have been postponing, and these could be clashing with family obligations. A conflict of interest between two people creates some emotional turmoil.

13 Today, someone may put the hard word on you, and you will have to sacrifice some of your time, energy and possibly even money to come to the party.

14 You can now investigate subjects that interested you some time ago, but which you never thought you were capable of studying. Think positively and go for your dreams!

15 Your mind will be opening up to the bigger picture today: towards philosophy and other psychological issues. Don't accept things at face value. Your thoughts are changing.

16 If you place too much emotional emphasis on a decision, the weight could cause it to collapse. Romance needs a careful balance of head and heart.

17 If you assume a high level of responsibility, your bosses or superiors are likely to give you a pat on the back for a job well done. Your confidence is strong today.

18 You will be astonished by the plentiful incidents happening in your peer group just now. Parties and other important social events seem predominant.

19 Your energies are bold and even a little abrasive. Sugar-coat what you say to get optimal results.

20 If you've been working hard, take some time out to enjoy your life with activities such as swimming, hiking, working out in the gym...or simply doing nothing at all.

21 It's best to get the small stuff out of the way early today! You are likely to make mountains out of molehills, especially if you're surrounded by reactive upstarts.

22 You can run but you can't hide, as they say. Today, you'll find the world is after you for even the most trivial things. Managing numerous requests will be annoying.

23 There's a shift away from your normally social instincts today, towards retreating from busy crowds. You will feel worn out. This is not a bad time to take stock of yourself and your relationships.

24 You'll mysteriously piece together some past incidents that you thought were totally unrelated. You'll solve a longstanding problem and possibly heal a relationship.

25 Your swift impulses and constructive responses to love are what are needed now. If you want to uphold a quality romance, you mustn't postpone a meeting or you'll miss a vital opportunity.

26 People often take things out of context, and this may be exactly what happens today. A word of encouragement or compliment may be taken the wrong way and rebound on you.

27 Family members feel as if you're disregarding them. Emotional blackmail will pull at your heartstrings, and their coercive talk will pull you away from your workaholic tendencies.

28 Underestimating the budget for a holiday is possible. Don't ruin your dream vacation or outing by underfunding it.

29 Something new will set your imagination on fire. Fear, as always, is the biggest obstacle in overcoming your search for excitement.

30 Big decisions sometimes take great courage. Longstanding friends or family members will feel threatened or angry if you choose to act without consulting them.

31 Don't exaggerate the benefits offered by a friend if they are associated with self-help. You know what you need to change in your life, so don't continue to play the victim.

2012
ASTRONUMEROLOGY

NICKNAMES STICK TO PEOPLE, AND
THE MOST RIDICULOUS ARE THE
MOST ADHESIVE.

Thomas C. Haliburton

THE POWER BEHIND YOUR NAME

It's hard to believe that your name resonates with a numerical vibration, but it's true! Simply by adding together the numbers of your name, you can see which planet rules you and what effects your name will have on your life and destiny. According to the ancient Chaldean system of numerology, each number is assigned a planetary energy, and each alphabetical letter a number, as in the following list:

AIQJY	=	1	Sun
BKR	=	2	Moon
CGLS	=	3	Jupiter
DMT	=	4	Uranus
EHNX	=	5	Mercury
UVW	=	6	Venus
OZ	=	7	Neptune
FP	=	8	Saturn
—	=	9	Mars

Note: The number 9 is not allotted a letter because it was considered 'unknowable'.

Once the numbers have been added, you can establish which single planet rules your name and personal affairs. At this point the number 9 can be used for interpretation. Do you think it's unusual that many famous actors, writers and musicians modify their names? This is to attract luck and good fortune, which can be made easier by using the energies of a friendlier planet. Try experimenting with the table and see how new names affect you. It's so much fun, and you may even attract greater love, wealth and worldly success!

Look at the following example to work out the power of your name. A person named Andrew Brown would calculate his ruling planet by correlating each letter to a number in the table, like this:

A N D R E W   B R O W N

1 5 4 2 5 6   2 2 7 6 5

And then add the numbers like this:

1 + 5 + 4 + 2 + 5 + 6 + 2 + 2 + 7 + 6 + 5   =   45

Then add   4 + 5   =   9

The ruling number of Andrew Brown's name is 9, which is governed by Mars (see how the 9 can now be used?). Now study the Name-Number Table to reveal the power of your name. The numbers 4 and 5 will play a secondary role in Andrew's character and destiny, so in his case you would also study the effects of Uranus (4) and Mercury (5).

Name Number	Ruling Planet	Name Characteristics
1	Sun	Attractive personality. Magnetic charm. Superman- or superwoman-like vitality and physical energy. Incredibly active and gregarious. Enjoys outdoor activities and sports. Has friends in powerful positions. Good government connections. Intelligent, spectacular, flashy and successful. A loyal number for love and relationships.
2	Moon	Feminine and soft, with an emotional temperament. Fluctuating moods but intuitive, possibly even has clairvoyant abilities. Ingenious nature. Expresses feelings kind-heartedly. Loves family, motherhood and home life. Night owl who probably needs more sleep. Success with the public and/or women generally.

Name Number	Ruling Planet	Name Characteristics
3	Jupiter	A sociable, optimistic number with a fortunate destiny. Attracts opportunities without too much effort. Great sense of timing. Religious or spiritual inclinations. Naturally drawn to investigating the meaning of life. Philosophical insight. Enjoys travel, explores the world and different cultures.
4	Uranus	Volatile character with many peculiar aspects. Likes to experiment and test novel experiences. Forward-thinking, with many extraordinary friends. Gets bored easily so needs plenty of inspiring activities. Pioneering, technological and creative. Wilful and obstinate at times. Unforeseen events in life may be positive or negative.

Name Number	Ruling Planet	Name Characteristics
5	Mercury	Sharp-witted and quick-thinking, with great powers of speech. Extremely active in life: always on the go and living on nervous energy. Has a youthful outlook and never grows old— looks younger than actual age. Has young friends and a humorous disposition. Loves reading and writing. Great communicator.
6	Venus	Delightful and charming personality. Graceful and eye-catching. Cherishes and nourishes friends. Very active social life. Musical or creative interests. Has great money-making opportunities as well as numerous love affairs. A career in the public eye is quite likely. Loves family, but often troubled over divided loyalties with friends.

Name Number	Ruling Planet	Name Characteristics
7	Neptune	Intuitive, spiritual and self-sacrificing nature. Easily duped by those who need help. Loves to dream of life's possibilities. Has healing powers. Dreams are revealing and prophetic. Loves the water and will have many journeys in life. Spiritual aspirations dominate worldly desires.
8	Saturn	Hard-working, ambitious person with slow yet certain achievements. Remarkable concentration and self-sacrifice for a chosen objective. Financially focused, but generous when a person's trust is gained. Proficient in his or her chosen field but a hard taskmaster. Demands perfection and needs to relax and enjoy life more.

Name Number	Ruling Planet	Name Characteristics
9	Mars	Extraordinary physical drive, desires and ambition. Sports and outdoor activities are major keys to health. Confrontational, but likes to work and play really hard. Protects and defends family, friends and territory. Has individual tastes in life, but is also self-absorbed. Needs to listen to others' advice to gain greater success.

YOUR PLANETARY RULER

Astrology and numerology are intimately connected. Each planet rules over a number between 1 and 9. Both your name and your birth date are governed by planetary energies. As described earlier, here are the planets and their ruling numbers:

1   Sun
2   Moon
3   Jupiter
4   Uranus
5   Mercury
6   Venus
7   Neptune
8   Saturn
9   Mars

To find out which planet will control the coming year for you, simply add the numbers of your birth date and the year in question. An example follows.

If you were born on 14 November, add the numerals 1 and 4 (14, your day of birth) and 1 and 1 (11, your month of birth) to the year in question, in this case 2012 (current year), like this:

Add 1 + 4 + 1 + 1 + 2 + 0 + 1 + 2 = 12

1 + 2 = 3

Thus, the planet ruling your individual karma for 2012 would be Jupiter, because this planet rules the number 3.

YOUR PLANETARY FORECAST

You can even take your ruling name number, as discussed previously, and add it to the year in question to throw more light on your coming personal affairs, like this:

A N D R E W B R O W N = 9

Year coming = 2012

Add 9 + 2 + 0 + 1 + 2 = 14

Add 1 + 4 = 5

Thus, this would be the ruling year number based on your name number. Therefore, you would study the influence of Mercury (5) using the Trends for Your Planetary Number table in 2012. Enjoy!

6 + 2012 = 11

1+1 = 2

Trends for Your Planetary Number in 2012

Year Number	Ruling Planet	Results Throughout the Coming Year
1	Sun	**Overview**

The commencement of a new cycle: a year full of accomplishments, increased reputation and brand new plans and projects.

Many new responsibilities. Success and strong physical vitality. Health should improve and illnesses will be healed.

If you have ailments, now is the time to improve your physical wellbeing—recovery will be certain.

Love and pleasure

A lucky year for love. Creditable connections with children, family life is in focus. Music, art and creative expression will be fulfilling. New romantic opportunities.

Work

Minimal effort for maximum luck. Extra money and exciting opportunities professionally. Positive new changes result in promotion and pay rises.

Improving your luck

Luck is plentiful throughout the year, but especially in July and August. The 1st, 8th, 15th and 22nd hours of Sundays are lucky.

Lucky numbers are 1, 10, 19 and 28.

Year Number	Ruling Planet	Results Throughout the Coming Year
2	Moon	

Overview

Reconnection with your emotions and past. Excellent for relationships with family members. Moodiness may become a problem. Sleeping patterns will be affected.

Love and pleasure

Home, family life and relationships are focused in 2012. Relationships improve through self-effort and greater communication. Residential changes, renovations and interior decoration bring satisfaction. Increased psychic sensitivity.

Work

Emotional in work. Home career, or hobby from a domestic base, will bring greater income opportunities. Females will be more prominent in your work.

Improving your luck

July will fulfil some of your dreams. Mondays will be lucky: the 1st, 8th, 15th and 22nd hours of them are the most fortunate. Pay special attention to the new and full Moons in 2012.

Lucky numbers include 2, 11, 20, 29 and 38.

Year Number	Ruling Planet	Results Throughout the Coming Year
3	Jupiter	

Overview

A lucky year for you. Exciting opportunities arise to expand horizons. Good fortune financially. Travels and increased popularity. A happy year. Spiritual, humanitarian and self-sacrificial focus. Self-improvement is likely.

Love and pleasure

Speculative in love. May meet someone new to travel with, or travel with your friends and lovers. Gambling results in some wins and some losses. Current relationships will deepen in their closeness.

Work

Fortunate for new opportunities and success. Employers are more accommodating and open to your creative expression. Extra money. Promotions are quite possible.

Improving your luck

Remain realistic, get more sleep and don't expect too much from your efforts. Planning is necessary for better luck. The 1st, 8th, 15th and 24th hours of Thursdays are spiritually very lucky for you.

Lucky numbers this year are 3, 12, 21 and 30. March and December are lucky months. The year 2012 will bring some unexpected surprises.

Year Number	Ruling Planet	Results Throughout the Coming Year
4	Uranus	

Overview

Unexpected events, both pleasant and sometimes unpleasant, are likely. Difficult choices appear. Break free of your past and self-imposed limitations. An independent year in which a new path will be forged. Discipline is necessary. Structure your life appropriately, even if doing so is difficult.

Love and pleasure

Guard against dissatisfaction in relationships. Need freedom and experimentation. May meet someone out of the ordinary. Emotional and sexual explorations. Spirituality and community service enhanced. Many new friendships.

Work

Progress is made in work. Technology and other computer or Internet-related industries are fulfilling. Increased knowledge and work skills. New opportunities arise when they are least expected. Excessive work and tension. Learn to relax. Efficiency in time essential. Work with groups and utilise networks to enhance professional prospects.

Year Number	Ruling Planet	Results Throughout the Coming Year

Improving your luck

Moderation is the key word. Be patient and do not rush things. Slow your pace this year, as being impulsive will only lead to errors and missed opportunities. Exercise greater patience in all matters. Steady investments are lucky.

The 1st, 8th, 15th and 20th hours of any Saturday will be very lucky in 2012.

Your lucky numbers are 4, 13, 22 and 31.

Year Number	Ruling Planet	Results Throughout the Coming Year
5	Mercury	

Overview

Intellectual activities and communication increases. Imagination is powerful. Novel and exciting new concepts will bring success and personal satisfaction.

Goal-setting will be difficult. Acquire the correct information before making decisions. Develop concentration and stay away from distracting or negative people.

Love and pleasure

Give as much as you take in relationships. Changes in routine are necessary to keep your love life upbeat and progressive. Develop open-mindedness.

Avoid being critical of your partner. Keep your opinions to yourself. Artistic pursuits and self-improvement are factors in your relationships.

Work

Become a leader in your field in 2012. Contracts, new job offers and other agreements open up new pathways to success. Develop business skills.

Speed, efficiency and capability are your key words this year. Don't be impulsive in making any career changes. Travel is also on the agenda.

Year Number	Ruling Planet	Results Throughout the Coming Year
		Improving your luck
		Write ideas down, research topics more thoroughly, communicate enthusiasm through meetings—this will afford you much more luck. Stick to one idea.
		The 1st, 8th, 15th and 20th hours of Wednesdays are luckiest, so schedule meetings and other important social engagements at these times.
		Throughout 2012 your lucky numbers are 5, 14, 23 and 32.

Year Number	Ruling Planet	Results Throughout the Coming Year
6	Venus	

Overview

A year of love. Expect romantic and sensual interludes, and new love affairs. Number 6 is also related to family life. Working with a loved one or family member is possible, with good results. Save money, cut costs. Share success.

Love and pleasure

The key word for 2012 is romance. Current relationships are deepened. New relationships will be formed and may have some karmic significance, especially if single. Spend time grooming and beautifying yourself: put your best foot forward. Engagement and even marriage is possible. Increased social responsibilities. Moderate excessive tendencies.

Work

Further interest in financial matters and future material security. Reduce costs and become frugal. Extra cash is likely. Additional income or bonuses are possible. Working from home may also be of interest. Social activities and work coincide.

Year Number	Ruling Planet	Results Throughout the Coming Year
		Improving your luck
		Work and success depend on a creative and positive mental attitude. Eliminate bad habits and personal tendencies that are obstructive. Balance spiritual and financial needs.
		The 1st, 8th, 15th and 20th hours on Fridays are extremely lucky this year, and new opportunities can arise when they are least expected.
		The numbers 6, 15, 24 and 33 will generally increase your luck.

Year Number	Ruling Planet	Results Throughout the Coming Year
7	Neptune	**Overview**

An intuitive and spiritual year. Your life path becomes clear. Focus on your inner powers to gain a greater understanding and perspective of your true mission in life. Remove emotional baggage. Make peace with past lovers who have hurt or betrayed you. Forgiveness is the key word this year.

Love and pleasure

Spend time loving yourself, not just bending over backwards for others. Sacrifice to those who are worthy. Relationships should be reciprocal. Avoid deception, swindling or other forms of gossip. Affirm what you want in a relationship to your lover. Set high standards.

Work

Unselfish work is the key to success. Learn to say no to demanding employers or co-workers. Remove clutter to make space for bigger and better things. Healing and caring professions may feature strongly. Use your intuition to manoeuvre carefully into new professional directions.

Year Number	Ruling Planet	Results Throughout the Coming Year
		Improving your luck
		Maintain cohesive lines of communication and stick to one path for best results. Pay attention to health and don't let stress affect a positive outlook. Sleep well, exercise and develop better eating habits to improve energy circulation.
		The 1st, 8th, 15th and 20th hours of Wednesdays are luckiest, so schedule meetings and other important social engagements at these times.
		Throughout 2012 your lucky numbers are 7, 16, 25 and 34.

Year Number	Ruling Planet	Results Throughout the Coming Year
8	Saturn	

Overview

This is a practical year requiring effort, hard work and a certain amount of solitude for best results. Pay attention to structure, timelines and your diary. Don't try to help too many people, but rather, focus on yourself. This will be a year of discipline and self-analysis. However, income levels will eventually increase.

Love and pleasure

Balance personal affairs with work. Show affection to loved ones through practicality and responsibility.

Dedicate time to family, not just work. Schedule activities outdoors for increased wellbeing and emotional satisfaction.

Work

Money is on the increase this year, but continued focus is necessary. Hard work equals extra income. A cautious and resourceful year, but be generous where possible. Some new responsibilities will bring success. Balance income potential with creative satisfaction.

Year Number	Ruling Planet	Results Throughout the Coming Year
		Improving your luck
		Being overcautious and reluctant to attempt something new will cause delay and frustration if new opportunities are offered. Be kind to yourself and don't overwork or overdo exercise. Send out positive thought-waves to friends and loved ones. The karmic energy will return.
		The 1st, 8th, 15th and 20th hours of Saturdays are the best times for you in 2012.
		The numbers 1, 8, 17, 26 and 35 are lucky.

Year Number	Ruling Planet	Results Throughout the Coming Year
9	Mars	

Overview

The ending of one chapter of your life and the preparation for the beginning of a new cycle. A transition period when things may be in turmoil or a state of uncertainty. Remain calm. Do not be impulsive or irritable. Avoid arguments. Calm communication will help find solutions.

Love and pleasure

Tremendous energy and drive help you achieve goals this year. But don't be too pushy when forcing your ideas down other people's throats, so to speak. Diplomatic discussions, rather than arguments, should be used to achieve outcomes. Discuss changes before making decisions with partners and lovers in your life.

Work

A successful year with the expectation of bigger and better things next year. Driven by work objectives or ambition. Tendency to overdo and overwork. Pace your deadlines. Leadership role likely. Respect and honour from your peers and employers.

Year Number	Ruling Planet	Results Throughout the Coming Year
		Improving your luck
		Find adequate outlets for your high level of energy through meditation, self-reflection and prayer. Collect your energies and focus them on one point. Release tension to maintain health.
		The 1st, 8th, 15th and 20th hours of Tuesdays will be lucky for you throughout 2012.
		Your lucky numbers are 9, 18, 27 and 36.

 *Mills & Boon® Online*

Discover more romance at
www.millsandboon.co.uk

- **FREE** online reads
- **Books** up to one month before shops
- **Browse our books** before you buy

...and much more!

For exclusive competitions and instant updates:

 Like us on **facebook.com/romancehq**

 Follow us on **twitter.com/millsandboonuk**

 Join us on **community.millsandboon.co.uk**

 Visit us Online — Sign up for our FREE eNewsletter at **www.millsandboon.co.uk**

WEB/M&B/RTL4

The World of Mills & Boon®

There's a Mills & Boon® series that's perfect for you. We publish ten series and with new titles every month, you never have to wait long for your favourite to come along.

Blaze — Scorching hot, sexy reads

By Request — Relive the romance with the best of the best

Cherish — Romance to melt the heart every time

Desire — Passionate and dramatic love stories

Browse our books before you buy online at **www.millsandboon.co.uk**

What will you treat yourself to next?

Ignite your imagination, step into the past…

INTRIGUE… Breathtaking romantic suspense

Captivating medical drama—with heart

MODERN™ International affairs, seduction and passion

nocturne™ Deliciously wicked paranormal romance

RIVA™ Live life to the full – give in to temptation

You can also buy Mills & Boon eBooks at **www.millsandboon.co.uk**

Visit us Online